Pamunkey Speaks.
Native Perspectives

By Kenneth Bradby Jr.

Conway Sams, "Conquest of Virginia," 1910

Edited by Bill O'Donovan

ISBN: 1-4196-5551-5

Design and production: Paula Pannoni
Photo credits: Front cover: Pamunkey River, Robin Lawson
Back cover: Rowboat, Barry Fitzgerald

To order additional copies, please contact us.
BookSurge Publishing
www.booksurge.com
1-866-308-6235 orders@booksurge.com

Contents

Why should you take by force that from us which you can have by love? Why should you destroy us who have provided you with food? What can you get by war? We can hide our provisions and fly into the woods. And then you must consequently famish by wrongdoing your friends.

What is the cause of your jealousy? You see us unarmed and willing to supply your wants if you come in a friendly manner; not with swords and guns as to invade an enemy.

Powhatan
as recorded by Capt. John Smith

Prologue

At the Treaty of Lancaster in Pennsylvania in 1744 between the leaders of the Six Nations and the royal colony of Virginia, the Virginia officials informed the Indians of a college in Williamsburg that would educate Indian youth. If the chiefs of the Six Nations would send six of their young braves to the college, the colony would provide for their proper education in the white ways.

In keeping with the native custom of not answering a serious proposition in haste, the Indians waited until the next day to express their appreciation at the kind offer, stating at length:

John Kahionhes Fadden

Meeting of the Six Nations.

"We know that you highly esteem the kind of learning taught in those colleges, and that the maintenance of our young men while with you would be very expensive to you.

"We are convinced, therefore, that you mean to do us good by your proposal, and we thank you heartily. But you who are wise must know that different nations have different conceptions of things, and you will therefore not take it amiss if our ideas of this kind of education happen not to be the same with yours.

"We have had some experience of it. Several of our young people were formally brought up at the colleges of the northern provinces and were instructed in all your sciences. But when they came back to

Smithsonian Institution
Paul Miles, Union Collins, George Cook.

us they were bad runners, ignorant of every means of living in the woods, unable to bear either cold or hunger. They knew neither how to build a cabin, take a deer, nor kill an enemy. They spoke our language imperfectly. They were, therefore, neither fit as hunters, warriors nor counselors.

They were totally good for nothing.

"We are not the less obliged by your kind offer. Though we decline accepting it, and to show our grateful sense of it, if the gentlemen of Virginia will send us a dozen of their sons we will take great care of their education, instruct them in all we know, and make men of them."

Chief Paul Miles and his wife Nannie.

Preface

When Captain John Smith landed in Jamestown in 1607, he was greeted by the indigenous members of the Powhatan confederacy of Native Americans. The central tribe of this confederacy, the Pamunkey Indians, has occupied the same tract of land since signing the treaty of 1677. The only other reservation in Virginia, the Mattaponi, is just a few miles away.

The Pamunkey have survived attempts to exterminate them physically, as when the English baited 200 of them into attending "peace talks" and murdered most of them

Family photo

George M. Cook in a print ad for the Indian Motorcyle Co.

with poisoned wine, then scalped the rest. The Virginia Company in London said the poisoned wine was a bit excessive. I'm not saying Indians were not guilty of equally violent behavior; I am saying there's a difference between invading and defending.

We've also survived the ravages of eugenics, when the first registrar of Virginia's Bureau of Vital Statistics, Walter Ashby Plecker, determined to eradicate any evidence of Indians in Virginia. A small-town doctor, in 1912 he began a campaign that lasted decades. He believed that anybody claiming to be Indian inherently had a mix of black blood because in Virginia one drop of black blood made an individual legally colored. Plecker thereby classified Indians as blacks. He ran Vital Statistics from 1912 to 1946.

Janet Fast

Techumseh Deerfoot Cook, known to all as Peach.

The "ancestral registration" provisions of the law were strictly enforced by Plecker. In 1925 he began requiring the U.S. Census Bureau to report *no* Indians in Virginia by 1930. The Census Bureau agreed to classify Virginia Indians with a footnote: "Includes a number of persons whose classification as Indians has been questioned." Plecker believed that all Indians had mingled their blood with free African Americans. He thus saw all Indians as colored people who were attempting to "pass."

Plecker went so far as to write in 1943 a list of surnames belonging to mixed-blood families who were suspected of having Negro ancestry who should not be allowed to pass as Indian or white, referring to us as "mongrels" (see later chapter).

Russell E. Booker Jr., Plecker's successor, called his treatment of Virginia's Native-American population during 1912-46 "documentary genocide."

Smithsonian Institution

Chief William Terrill Bradby, 1893 Chicago World Expo.

As to the celebrated rescue of John Smith by Pocahontas, Michael Lind wrote in the New Republic (1995): "J.A. Lemay, in 'Did Pocahontas Save Captain John Smith?' (1992), argues that Smith's rescue by Pocahontas took place more or less as he described it."

Lind continued: "Unlike the tale of Smith's rescue, the story of Pocahontas's later marriage to John Rolfe never became popular during the centuries in which interracial marriage was not only the greatest taboo in the United States but illegal in most parts of the country. In 1924 the Virginia legislature revised the state's anti-miscegenation law, which dated from the 1600s, to exempt proud white descendants of Pocahontas (who included Woodrow Wilson's second wife, Edith Bolling Galt): 'persons who have one-sixteenth or less of the blood of the American Indian and have no other non-Caucasian blood shall be deemed to be white persons.' This defini-tion would have

Virginia State Library

Jimmy Bradby in center boat, others unidentified.

excluded the Indian princess herself. Had she and Rolfe married in the Old Dominion in 1967, they would have com-mitted a felony."

This project relies on oral histories given by relatives and friends as well as hours of research. Caroline Bradby Cook, my great-great-grandmother, bore a great chief, George Major Cook, who, among other things shook the hands of several Virginia governors and at least one presi-dent. He was a noted proponent of civil rights for Native

Americans (no mean feat in the early 20th century) and once fainted outright on a courtroom floor during an impassioned defense of a tribal member accused of shoplifting a dress.

His second daughter was my grandmother Dora. She was a kind, deeply religious woman whose care-worn face nonetheless expressed her joy in life. She loved nothing better than to prepare Sunday dinner for the family. Afterward my dad would push himself away from the table, saying, "Momma, you've certainly outdone yourself. Everything was delicious!" Modestly, she would reply, "Well, thank you, but that was probably the worst pie I ever made." She sang in church with my aunts Ruth and Bernice, as well as cousin Daisy.

Barry Fitzgerald, Fredericksburg Free-Lance Star
Chief Tecumseh Deerfoot Cook, 1973.

Her husband Jimmy was quiet and industrious. If he caught you looking at him for more than a few seconds, he would lightly chuckle and you would sense that he knew far more than he let on. He would take me out on his boat and after 10 or 15 minutes stop the motor and say, "Throw your line right there." Every time, I'd catch a big old catfish. He knew that river. My dad, Ken Bradby, said when Grandpa worked during the Depresson as caretaker of an estate called Lester Manor just outside the reservation, he would often sneak bags of food out to the poorer folks working on the grounds who were having trouble feeding their families. I wish I had talked with him more when he was alive, but I suspect he pretty much said what he had to say and that was it.

My grandmother's brother was Tecumseh Deerfoot Cook, known to all as Peach, chief for 42 years until his retirement with the onset of his wife's Alzheimer's disease. He lived to be 103 and was the epitome of respectability. He was set in his convictions and lived and led by example.

Once when Peach was about 90, I was smoking on the steps of the Pottery School, just beside the Museum conference room where the entire tribe was having a dinner for some occasion. Peach walked over and saw the cigarette in my hand, scowled and said,

Family photo

Author's grandmother, Dora Cook Bradby.

"You know, I smoked until I was 59 and gave it up just like that." I replied "Well in that case I better quit in the next 20 years if I want to make it to 90." The look on his face went from disapproval to anger. Like a child chastised, I put out

Uncle Peach dances at his 100th birthday celebration.

the smoke. He commanded respect by his mere presence.

These are treasures among the memories of my childhood. Now it is 30 years later, and most of the elder folks have gone. I feel there is a need to record an account of the memories and thoughts of the people of Pamunkey, before it's too late.

On Family Life

Joyce Bradby Krigsvold: Momma (Dora) used to talk about how they would have people come over to her daddy's (George Major Cook) house for Sunday dinner. Because he was chief, they always had people over for dinner. Grandma (Theodora) would cook, but the kids couldn't eat yet. They had to wait for the grown-ups to finish. Momma would wait with them as the grown-ups kept eating and eating, and the kids would get what was left over. Sometimes it wasn't much, maybe a cold biscuit or something.

Family photo

Peach and Dora Cook.

One time, there was a big old kettle of soup cooking outside, and a duck fell into the kettle. Grandma just plucked the duck out of the kettle and kept on cooking the soup. It's a wonder more people didn't die from things like that back then.

Russell Bradby: I had a good mom and dad. We always went to church. I had a good father, a good Christian man. And I'm glad I did. He didn't smoke or chew nothing. You couldn't even say "hell" around him. My sisters Ruth and Bernice wanted to go dancing, he wouldn't want that. We used to have dances down there. I remember that. I was young, the youngest one of them all. There were nine of us. One brother died when he was 18.

Downstairs we had a great big round wood stove. We slept upstairs. "Morning!" Daddy would holler. "Work's ready!" We'd be a long time coming down. About the third time he hollered, we'd hear feet coming up stairs, and we jumped out of bed and flew down the stairs. Everybody gathered around that stove.

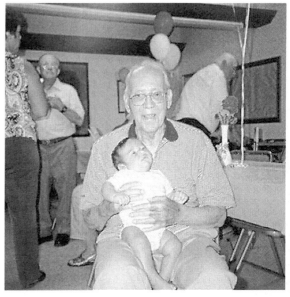

Family photo

Russell Bradby with his grandnephew River Cook.

Kevin Brown: Peach told me that one time he was in an outhouse when a black widow spider bit him on the privates. They could hear him in the house hollering from the outhouse. People across the road heard him hollering. His sister Pocahontas happened to be there, I think she was down from Philadelphia visiting, and she had some pills for pain.

It calmed him down before they took him to the hospital. The doctor said if they hadn't given him those pills, he would have probably died. It was something to calm his nerves, and the spider bite attacks your central nervous system, so since he was drugged up, it didn't affect him as bad.

Peach and Grampa (Ed) were like best buddies when they were younger. They were about the same age, Peach was about a year or two older. I guess they were about the only kids that age, so they used to hang out together. Peach used to work for Jim Bradby. He used to pay him for hoeing corn. Grampa and Peach were out at Swett's Landing hoeing corn one time,

Smithsonian Institution

Tecumseh Cook, mending fishing nets.

thinning it out. Grampa had some chewing tobacco and gave Peach a piece. Peach never chewed tobacco before, so he swallowed it and got sick. Grampa said he was turning green and had to carry him all the way from Swett's up to his house. Peach was afraid to tell his folks he'd been chewing tobacco, so he told them he had just come down with a fever.

His mother sent Peach's brother "Sweet" out to the pocket to where there were big poplar trees to get poplar leaves to put on his head and cool his fever down. They were scared about rheumatic fever that was going around those days. But he was just scared to get a whipping because he was chewing tobacco.

Peach's sister Cap (Captola Cook) told me about how they found Major Cook (George M. Cook's father) floating in the river, drowned. He had long black hair. They couldn't see him, but they saw his hair floating on the water. They reached down and pulled it up and it was him. And they lived right there, in front of that field by Jim Bradby's house, in a log cabin. So that's where the relationship between the Bradbys and the Cooks was, because they shared some of that common area. George's mother, Caroline, was Jim Bradby Sr.'s aunt.

Family photo

Captola Cook, or Aunt Cap.

Margaret Dickerson: We had the only phone for 15 miles around, so if anyone needed a doctor they would come to us. We had the phone in the dining room. Well, it was Christmas Eve when we always had oyster stew. It was so delicious. My mother said, "We have to eat so Margaret can take her bath."

There was a knock at the door and it was Effie Collins. She said there was a problem and asked if she could use the telephone. Daddy said, "Yes, come on in. You know where it is." She came in and said, "I don't know the number of the sheriff. I have to call the sheriff." And Daddy said, "Why? It's Christmas Eve." And she replied, "Archie's dead."

Daddy was so distressed! "How did he die?" he asked. She said,

Family photo

Archie Collins as a youngster.

"Because I killed him." Mother and Daddy were speechless. Finally he asked, 'Well, how did you kill him?' She replied, "With a railroad tie. He made me mad. There was an old rotten railroad tie. I picked it up and hit him in the head, and now I have to call the sheriff."

Daddy gave her the sheriff's number and she called him, and finally the sheriff came since he lived 10 miles away.

Daddy knew the sheriff well. When he got there he asked, "Where is your husband?" and she said, "Down on the railroad tracks." He said, "Well, it's dark and I don't have any lights. Mr. Dickerson, will you walk with me?" And my daddy didn't want to, but he did. They found the body and called the undertaker.

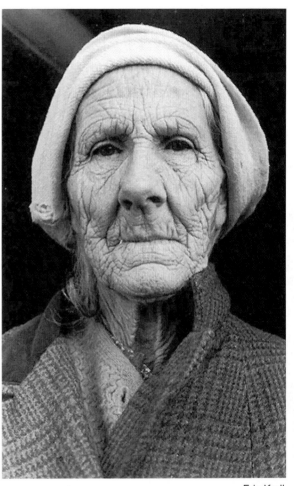

Eric Kroll

Effie Collins.

They arrested Effie and they took her to the little jail in King William County. Then they called the chief, who I think was Paul Miles. I still hadn't had my dinner or my bath, and my mother was very nervous. Early Christmas morning, the chief came to the house and wanted my father to ride with him to the courthouse and see Effie. The Indians on the reservation had collected some money for the bond, and she was released from jail. They took her back to the reservation, and someone had her over for dinner. She never spent a night in jail. When the trial came, who was the first witness for

Effie? My daddy. My mother was so upset, but in the end, Effie went free. I don't guess she was ever punished in any way, because she lived on the reservation practically forever."

Kevin Brown: Grampa (Ed Bradby, Jimmy's brother) used to bring in white ash wood that they cut in the low grounds. As a young man, he'd go over in a boat with other men, past Swett's Landing and cut wood with a crosscut saw. They'd cut it six or seven feet long and put it in the bow of the boat to row it back to shore in the front of the house. They had a sawhorse there and cut it up into stove-sized pieces, so there was always a woodpile there by the well.

Family photo

Kevin Brown.

One night when it was starting to get dark, his mother kept yelling after him to go and get the wood. He kept fooling around and then it was almost dark. He went and got an armload of wood. When he turned around and started coming into the house he saw a *devil* sitting on the front porch.

He said he was there plain as day, sitting on his haunches, with hooves for hands and feet. He was covered in fur like a deer. He was brown and had short pointy ears and blue beady eyes. And he had a tail, a forked tail wrapped over his shoulder.

Grampa dropped the wood and ran over to the barn where the hog pen was. When he came back the devil was gone, so he hurried and brought the wood inside. After that, whenever his mother told him to bring in the wood, he did it as soon as she told him. Wouldn't wait til dark.

Family photo

George Cook.

On Poverty

Joyce Bradby Krigsvold: Momma said they never had shoes in the summer, but always managed to have all the kids in shoes by school time. I don't know how they did it. At Christmas, maybe all they would get is an orange and a penny, but they thought that was the best Christmas ever.

Kevin Brown: My Grandpa (Ed Bradby) started fishing when he was five years old. His father made him a pair of white pine oars that were seven foot long. They were light, so he could row the boat with them. He used to row the boat all the way down to the mussel pond, three times a day at — at five years old. They rowed three miles each way and then threw the nets out. That's why his arms were so big. He would work all spring long, and his

Family photo

Children of George M. Cook, circa 1900.

Jimmy Bradby, (bottom left) and family. Next to him, Russell & Ed, are subjects in this book.

father (Jim Bradby Sr.) would pay him a nickel's worth of ginger snaps. Fish three times a day for three months straight and get a nickel's worth of ginger snaps. And eat the profits up in about five minutes.

Russell Bradby: I remember back in the '30s when times were tight. I used to work picking apples for a guy. We got 10 cents an hour 10 hours a day for five and a half days a week, so that's a $5 dollar bill and 50 cents a week. We had to walk three or four miles just to get to the truck to take us to work! We had it tough. We really did. We didn't know we was poor, because everybody was poor back then. We thought we was getting along pretty good. After I got out and got in the world, I seen how poor we was.

Louis Stewart: The government put out a Works Progress Administration program for poor people in Franklin Roosevelt's time. We dug up roots, mainly. Then they came up with the Civilian Conservation Corps, where you made $30 a month but had to send it home. Me, Everett and Cleve did it for 18 weeks. But we always beat the check home (laughing). Cleve always got along pretty good. He was cutting hair in that CCC camp and doing everything. When we got out of there, Everett went up to Philadelphia and got killed. He fell 22 stories on a work site. He was a carpenter and he climbed too high. He had a piece of plywood and the wind caught hold of him. He would have been the same age as Russell if he lived, 91 or 92. But them things happen.

Ken Bradby Jr.

Louis Stewart.

From a Smithsonian Institution field report: The level of poverty at Pamunkey in the early 20th century is reflected in the toys and recreation the children participated in.

Crude spinning tops provided hours of entertainment. They were made from cutting the rim off simple spools and inserting pegs of wood in the center hole and spinning by hand. Another common toy was the alder bark "pop gun." With the pith pushed out, it was capable of shooting cedar berry "bullets." Circular slices of red oak called "tanbark" are threaded and the ends tied to form a circle. With a finger at either end, the disc is spun until the slack tightened, the hands are brought together and spread apart. The wooden disc actually hums. This was known as a "buzz saw."

Smithsonian Institution

Theodora Cook, wife of Chief George M. Cook.

When Frank Speck of the Smithsonian came to the reservation in 1915, Chief George M. Cook showed him a "mysterious" windmill toy. It was an eight-inch piece of wood with two dozen notches on the upper side. On the end was a two-inch revolving blade attached to a nail in the stick. With the toy in hand, the notches are rubbed with another stick in the other hand. The blade magically revolves to the left or right, by pressure applied to the sides of the stick. Pressing with the thumb while grating with the other stick makes the blade goes one way, while when he presses his fingers on the other side, it changes direction.

John Dennis, the Chief's brother-in-law, and in his 80s the oldest man on the reservation, showed Speck an example of a functional toy crossbow.

Other children's games included "Club fist," similar to the way kids choose up sides in baseball, where players put one fist on top of the

Peach as a young man, with his dog Colonel.

previous player, until all players are in. A player who is designated "It" says, "What you got there?"

The player on top replies, "Club fist."

"Well, take it off or I'll knock it off!"

This is repeated until only one fist remains. It says,

Theodora and Chief George M. Cook with their children, 1899. His mother is standing in back.

"What you got there?"

"Piece of cheese."

"Where's my share?"

"Cat got it."

"Where's the cat?"

"In the woods."

"Where's the woods?"

"Fire burned it."

"Where's the fire?"

"Water squenched it."

"Where's the water?"

"Ox drank it."

"Where's the ox?"

"Butcher killed it."

"Rope hung him."

"Where's the rope?"

"Rat gnawed it."

"Where's the rat?"

"Cat caught him."

"Where's the cat?"

"Dead and buried behind the church door, and now first one who shows his teeth gets ten pinches."

Then It tries to make the other players show their teeth by laughing or speaking.

All this was described by Mrs. George M. Cook. She also recalled a "Counting out" game where players hold out index fingers next to their neighbors while someone designated "It" spells them out with this verse:

William Attrivity,

He's a good fisherman.

Catches fishes,

Puts 'em in dishes.

Catches hens,

Puts 'em in pens.

Smithsonian Institution

Theodora Dennis Cook, wife of George Major Cook.

Some lay eggs,
Some lay none.
Wire. Briar.
Limberlock.
Sit and sing till 12 o'clock.
Clock fell down,
Mouse ran 'round.
O-U-T spells out!
The player who is spelled out must run around on tiptoe, and if one sound is heard by the other players he must start all over again.

Mrs. Cook recalled: "We used to have a lot of fun with that because some could tiptoe, and some couldn't."

Games played by adults at parties included "Spinning the plate," whereby a player spins a tin plate and calls the name of the player who must catch the plate before it stops, or pay a forfeit.

Family photo

John Dennis with unidentified child, probably his daughter.

On Education

Classes at the Indian School on the Pamunkey Reservation were taught during the session of 1909-1910 by Miss Agnes Lumsden and during 1910-1911 by Mrs. Lucie B. Dudley.

A good one-room schoolhouse was erected on the reservation during the fall of 1909, with the Indians themselves furnishing the rough lumber and much of the labor. The house is neatly painted and is provided with the latest approved system of heat and ventilation. It has slate blackboards and good furniture. Two acres of ground were secured, and the sanitary conveniences were carefully provided for. This school, as well as the schools at the two state

Smithsonian Institution

One-room schoolhouse was erected in 1909.

reformatories, are under immediate control and management of the Virginia Board of Education and are supervised by the Secretary of the Board. (Virginia School Report 1913:30.)

— From a 2007 petition to Congress seeking federal recognition.

Louis Stewart: I was born in 1916. We had a rough time coming up. My brothers, my sisters and the Dennises (Tom, Irma, Richard and Edith Collins) all went to Robert Fulton School in Richmond. I think I made it up to the third or fourth grade before they kicked us all out. Said we had too much black blood in us. So I came here and I went into this school over here (pointing to the old Pamunkey schoolhouse). Then they opened up an Indian school near Fulton, and we went there.

Ken Bradby Jr.

Robert Fulton School in Richmond, Virginia, where Pamunkey Indians were expelled in the 1920s due to race issues.

There was a black school two blocks down the road from the Fulton school, and there was the white school So you had the Indian school, a black school and a white school. See what I mean? Now, the Dennises wouldn't go to the Indian

This is an Indian school in the Fulton district of Richmond in the 1920s. Louis Stewart has his pants rolled up.

school. They was too proud. They went to the Catholic school. My wife went to the Fulton school, but she was six years younger than me. But she didn't mind no difference, you know. She loved Indians (laughing).

CHIEF OF PAMUNKEY INDIANS AT POKIE POW WOW
Chief George Cook Makes
Splendid Address Before
Pocahontas Literary Club
– Article from the "Grapurchat" student
newspaper at Radford Teaching College, 1924

Twelve "moons" had come and gone since the tribe of Pocahontas had gathered, one and all, to welcome old members, friends and visitors. Feb. 23 was set apart as the day of homecoming for the year 1924.

Former members were sent special invitations. Excitement and curiosity prevailed, for this pow wow was to be a departure from the usual regime. We were to have Chief Cook of the Pamunkey tribe as our speaker and guest of honor.

The rising curtain revealed a lovely forest scene with tall pine trees shrouded in shadows. From these trees came a stately figure, a girl dressed in the symbolical costume of purple and gray representing our alma mater. She advanced slowly and with graceful pantomime ease called Mary Draper Ingalls and Pocahontas to her. In the still shadows, with only the soft glow of the footlights to illuminate the figures, the pantomime was complete. All three retreated, the two brave heroines feeling the sublime approbation of their dear school.

Smithsonian Institution

Pamunkey School, 1890s.

Light flooded the stage as Pocahontas returned with the Indian chieftain. She followed in the wake of the figures preceding her, leaving the chief with his audience.

What an inspiring figure he was! We felt as if an Indian chief whom we had silently admired in some picture had suddenly material-ized into flesh and blood, so nearly had he resembled a picture. His long, black hair was adorned with a band of feathers. A serviceable and much-valued buckskin suit beautifully trimmed with fringe and the most intricate beadwork did duty for "best wear" on this occasion. Wearing a belt

Smithsonian Institution

Union Collins and Pocahontas Cook, two students at the Pamunkey schoolhouse.

elaborately fitted with knives in sheathes and supporting a medicine bag which rested on one hip while holding a spear in one hand and a peace pipe in the other, this man presented to us the typical first American.

Could he speak intelligently, this representative of a fast disappearing race? Most emphatically, yes! His words, combined with his splendid delivery, held the audience while he

Julia Kyle (standing center) presides over her students.

related the story of the coming of the white man. He pictured the steady retreat of the Red Man into the forests spoke of Indian massacres and English victories.

There was scarcely a complaint of the injustice of the matter as the narrator told how the different tribes in Virginia had been reduced to only 196 persons under the tribal form of government in his tribe at Lester Manor. Under the circumstances one could not but admire the independence, loyalty and fidelity shown by this Native American clinging to his family traditions and ideals.

As the speaker completed his story and stepped back, he

Dora Cook and her sister Pocahontas.

was met with such an applause by his appreciative audience that he followed with an encore, a beautiful legend of Indian corn. The special music was a very enjoyable texture.

The final scenes were clear, vivid and expressive. The past was faithfully portrayed by a pantomime that presented a campfire watched by an Indian chief and two of his braves. The effectiveness of the scene was again enhanced by semi-darkness. All was peaceful until the sound of a footstep announced the coming of a stranger.

Immediately the Indians retreated to the forest, their hearts filled with terror. They covertly watched from the protection of the trees while George Washington approached their deserted campfire. Meditatively he surveyed the scene, noting the burning embers. At this moment the chief stepped from his hiding place and saluted the stranger. The braves were called and all four seated themselves around the fire to smoke the pipe of peace.

After the program a reception was held in Pocahontas Hall to which all members, faculty, and visitors were invited. Everyone felt that this third annual pow wow was a happy success.

Margaret Dickerson: Julia Kyle, the teacher on the reservation, was really nice. She lived with Willie and Daisy Bradby at his mother Luzeilia's house from September to June. Julia went home at Christmas to Cumberland County. Her husband had been dead for years and years, and she had no children. I think that when I was little, her mother was still living. But she would teach and then go home for the

Smithsonian Institution

George Major Cook.

summer, and for Christmas.

I don't know how long she taught on the reservation, but it was a long, long time. I'm sure there's a record of it somewhere. When she retired, my mother was asked to teach. My mother told them no because she had not taught since I had been born and by then I was already in college. She was heavily involved in her church and helped my dad at the store, and she just couldn't do it. Finally they came back and said they just couldn't find a teacher. So she would take it just for a month. She told them, "I can

Family photo

Dora Bradby and Daisy Stewart Bradby, potters.

get them enrolled, get them their books, give them their assignments, get the parents acquainted, just during September."

Well, at the end of September, the chief, that would have been Paul Miles, and the superintendent of instruction, a man named Paschal who grew up with my dad, came and had a conversation with my mom and dad, and she agreed to continue until Thanksgiving. But her daughter, me, was in the second year of college and I would be coming home for Christmas, and she wanted to do things with me over Christmas. She ended up staying from September 1942 until June 1960.

Joyce Bradby Krigsvold recalls when her brother, Ken Bradby, was sent on a train to attend school in Kansas at the age of 12:

Family photo

Joyce Bradby Krigswold with Ken Livingstone, mayor of London, 2007

That was always sad. All through those years, every year we had to drive to Richmond. I remember we would take him to a place called Ahab's Restaurant, then we'd take him to the train station and see him off. Mama would start to cry, but it had to be done.

To allow him to go to a non-white school would be like saying the state was right with the Jim Crow laws. And we were Indians, so he was going go to an Indian school. It was as simple as that. When he came back after graduating, that was a great time. He would always take us to Richmond to the rock and roll shows. Chuck Berry, Fabian, all those guys. It was a really good time.

Family photo

Kenneth Bradby Sr. (right), was forced to board a train at age 12 to attend school in Kansas due to racial integrity laws.

On Pottery Making

–From a 1987 documentary, "The Old Ways: The Pamunkey Indian Women's Pottery Guild," narrated by Kenneth Bradby Sr.

Bernice Bradby Langston, Dora Cook Bradby, Daisy Stewart Bradby, Irma Allmond Page, Willis Almond Bradley. In the spring of 1987, these are the members of the Pamunkey Indians' Women Pottery Guild.

State Road 673, once an ancient footpath, leads west to the Pamunkey Indian Reservation past the York & Richmond Railroad built in 1854. Past Cohoke Creek with

From an old postcard

Pamunkey potters Ruth Cook, Mary Bradby, Bernice Bradby Langston, Daisy Stewart Bradby and Dora Bradby in the old school building, 1974. It was called the Trading Post after integration into public schooling.

its falls, past creeks and marshes, past fields and farmlands.

In ancient days, the tribe of the great Powhatan Confederacy numbered more than 9,000. Today the Pamunkey have fewer than 80 persons living on the reservation. This land of almost 1,000 acres was deeded to the tribe in the late 17th century, but ancestors of the Pamunkey tribe date to prehistoric times. In 1607 John Smith, exploring the waterways of eastern Virginia, wrote in his chronicle "Travels and Works": "Where the river is divided, the land is called Pamunkey."

Family photo

Pocahontas Cook and Katie Bradby Southard performing at the New York World's Fair, 1939.

On this day, after weeks of unusually high tide, tribal member Herman Dennis has offered to dig clay for the pottery guild members. This clay deposit has been in documented use for the last 200 years. It is probable that clay has been dug here ever since the community was founded. In earlier times, the opening of a clay mine was a great feast day for the whole tribe.

Dora, Daisy, Bernice and Irma inspect the clay and are

Women's Pottery Guild, 1940s, where they sold pottery when the school was still functional. The log cabin burned down, but the chimney still stands.

pleased with its texture and quality. When all the buckets are filled with clay, Herman marks the digging place. He unloads the clay outside the pottery school. The clay will be dried and stored for later use.

On this warm spring day, Daisy and Dora prepare their work. The dried clay is pounded into coarse particles and placed in water. The mixture is stirred, then sieved into a separate container to remove pebbles and bits of shell. The slip formed in this process, thickened but still liquid, is slowly poured onto a plaster bat to set. When the edges dry, Daisy easily rolls the clay off the batt, forming a rough mound, or "wedge." The clay has firmed and is now ready for use in shaping pottery.

Dora, working from a block of freshly prepared clay, begins the base and the first coil of her pot. Coil construction is a traditional method, used by pottery makers over many hundreds of years. As each coil is rolled and added, Dora carefully seals the inner and outer surfaces with her finger-

Family photo

Dora Cook Bradby, the author's grandmother.

tips. Small clay modeling implements, as well as clam and mussel shells, are used to scrape and seal the walls of the pot and to create a texture on the surface.

Examples of Pamunkey-made pottery are placed in the museum for sale to visitors and collectors. Each artist works individually and at her own pace, for there is no sense here of haste or impatience. Working hours are regular and seasonal. When summer approaches, pottery guild members will have home gardens to plant and tend in preparation for the winter.

Daisy rolls and stretches her clay into a long coil. The coil is set in place to widen and open the vessel that she is making. The bowl is smoothed and turned upside down. A small kitchen knife is used to refine the base and outer wall of the pot. A damp sponge aids in the smoothing process. Daisy strengthens the surface using a small wooden paddle.

Molded glazed ware is also produced and sold by the Pottery Guild. Visitors to the museum are attracted by the color and variety of traditional decorative objects. Fish, animals, birds, plates, bowls and vases are almost always small. So they are less costly than the coil-built pots.

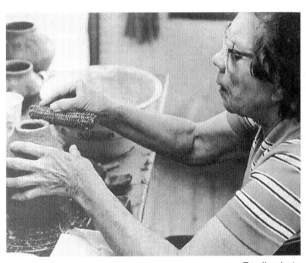

Family photo

Katie Bradby Southard.

Bernice skillfully applies layers of colors to form the scales of a fish. Firing will deepen and enhance each layer. This piece and similar objects will be fired in an electric kiln. The following day, Bernice will brush on several layers of pink glaze. When fired, pieces glazed in this manner produce vivid colors with a high glossy finish.

Irma and Willis concentrate on the final modeling process. With a wide, flattened coil, Irma elongates the neck of her pot to achieve a purity of line that characterizes the work of Pamunkey craft women. Irma and Willis use pot-

Pamunkey Museum opened in 1979.

ter's wheels in this process. Irma incises a simple geometric design around the nearly completed pot. Almost classic in feeling, designs such as this are shared by Indian artists throughout the country. Daisy has adorned the neck of her pot with the head of a young Indian boy. Her fingers deepen the contours of the face, and add details which create a distinctive personality. The hair is drawn using a wooden modeling tool.

The final step before firing is burnishing. Dora works the surface of her pot with the tip of an antler. This process, depending on the size of the vessel, can take many hours. Willis refines the spaces between her incised design with a flat-tipped modeling tool. Daisy has finished and burnished her pot. She rubs and polishes the surface evenly. A light crosshatched design has been added.

On firing day, all the pieces have been placed in the sun to warm while Daisy prepares the fire. Only hardwoods are used in this process. A rectangular brick kiln has been con-

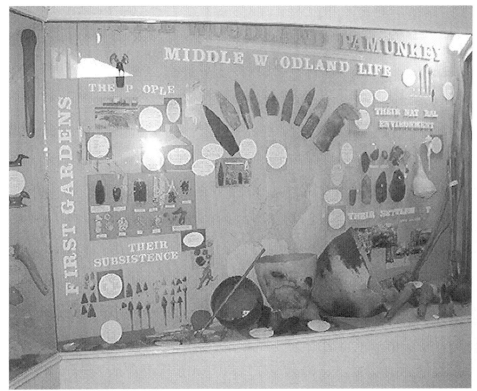

Diorama inside Pamunkey Museum depicts the early years.

structed near the pottery. When the fire is ready, the pots are loosely filled with pine tags of dried needles and carefully placed in the kiln. The pine tags ignite quickly, blackening and hardening the interior of the pots. Armloads of pine tags are heaped over the pieces to be fired. Quickly, sheets of tin are placed over the kiln to contain the heat and smother the flames. Smoke seeps from under the tin as the pots cook.

The women of the pottery guild remain near the kiln to observe and check on the firing process. The pots are inspected as 4½ hours pass. No exact time for firing can be calculated. Weather, time of day and the season are all a part of the process. A sense of anticipation accompanies the completion of the firing time. Dora is the first to take her pot from the still-smoldering ashes as each woman in turn follows until the pots are picked from the kiln and carefully examined. The color of the fired pot is often surprising. Uneven firing can sometimes produce pinkish clouding of the surface. Discoloration can be evened out and darkened by re-firing, should the artist choose to do so.

From a school in Richmond, 46 students and their teachers have come to the reservation today on a field trip. They will explore Pamunkey history and visit the pottery school and museum. Each year, hundreds of students learn traditional pottery-making techniques in this manner. On these

Smithsonian Institution

James E. Bradby overseeing Paul Miles digging clay.

occasions, guild members wear Native American costumes. The children delight in seeing real Indians working the moist clay and in listening to tribal stories. Bernice tells the well remembered story of John Smith and the young Indian princess Pocahontas. The children finish their lunch outdoors near the old school building.

For many years, Pamunkey students have been bused far away to King William Courthouse to attend the county schools. The wonders of the Pamunkey museum, opened in 1979, orient the children to the Pamunkey world. Hundreds of artifacts, in well designed displays, tell the history of the Pamunkey people from prehistoric times to the present day. Before leaving, the children are allowed to shop for small gifts and curios in the museum gift shop.

Income from the gift shop is important for upkeep and repair of the museum and pottery school. These remembrances of the old ways will keep their Pamunkey adventure alive, helping to pass on to growing minds the traditions of the Pamunkey women's pottery guild.

Family photo

Joyce Bradby Krivsvold with infant River Cook.

Joyce Bradby Krigsvold: We used to go down to the pottery and watch Momma and them making pottery, but we didn't have any interest in making pottery back then. We'd listen to them talk, but we weren't interested. Later on in the

Willie Bradby and Tecumseh Cook mending shad net.

'40s, the kids in the school had to take pottery classes, but we didn't when I was in school.

To get the clay for pottery, they had to find it in the riverbank, dig it out and put it in big buckets. Then we'd take the clay to the pottery school and put it in big bins to let it dry out.

They would pound it out into small particles and add water. They would stir it and keep adding liquid to it. It takes about three days to get it to about the consistency of cream.

Then they would strain it, and get all of the pebbles and sand and rocks out. They'd pour it on a plaster of paris batt (a large round plate-like object), and it would take about 20 minutes to harden to where we could roll it off the batt into a ball.

Lester Manor, where Richard McCluney grew up.

That's the clay they would work with. The liquid clay, called slip, was what they used to make the molds from. But the balls of clay are what they used to make the reddish glazed pottery and black pottery. The pottery for sale at the Dog Mart in Fredericksburg was always the reddish orange-glazed pottery. I'm not sure exactly when they started making black pottery. I was living in Texas, so I guess it was in the '70s.

Kevin Brown: I took pottery when I was in high school in Pennsylvania. One of my neighbors was a professional potter who had a studio. I used to work pottery after school there, so I already knew how before I came to the reservation. I started working with the potters on the reservation, and I was in the Pottery Guild. They were doing their hand-built stuff, but I was doing wheel pottery. I used to dig clay for them every year. Ernest (Jim Bradby Jr.'s brother) used to dig it before me. When he died, I took over. I dug it I guess for about five or six years, then Herman Dennis took over from me. They've dug most of it up now. It's hard to find these days.

Ed Bradby: I must have been about 14 years old when we first got a motorboat. They sold gas at Lester Manor out of a 50-gallon drum. Well, I didn't know about gasoline, nobody else knew about it around here. There was no such thing as gas lawnmowers back then. The cows and horses grazed the grass. We traveled by horse and buggy.

So my dad sent me to Lester Manor by boat to get a gallon of gas. It was kept about a hundred yards from the store. This was in May, and it was hot. I had to row a boat to Lester Manor, and I stopped about 300 yards before reaching it. I was too doggone lazy to row all the way there, so I put the anchor out and I walked. He gave me the gallon of gas, and I walked down

Smithsonian Institution

Aubrey Stewart, Louis's brother, from the 1920s.

and put the gas in the boat. But coming down the hill, I wasted a little gas. I don't know what I had it in, but the container evidently wasn't tight. I often heard people say how gasoline would burn, you know? I put the gas in my boat and went back and lit the gasoline. Figured on puttin' it out when it started. I just wanted to see how fast it would burn. But when I threw that match in the gasoline, it went WHOOOOP! And in two minutes' time, it was lickin' the tops of the pine trees.

Family photo

Mary Bradby, Ruth Cook, Daisy Bradby.

I got scared and I came home and didn't say nothin' about it. The dog-gone whole woods was on fire. They had to close down Lester Manor store and all around there to fight the fire all afternoon.

Well, my dad had sent me fishing for herring that afternoon. I had to go up the river about two or three miles. There happened to be two black men fishing up by Lester Manor, and they said that when the fire started there happened to be a white boat that left about the same time. They traced it down to me. The next morning, I was shipping a load of fish into Lester Manor when the owner of the store came up to me and said, "How did that fire get away from you yesterday, boy?" And I told him the truth. I meant to put it out right away, but it got away from me. I didn't have no right to light it.

That guy didn't have no time for me after that. He couldn't forgive me. But they are the little things that happened to me because I was curious. I wanted to know what was what. I wanted to know if gasoline would burn, how fast it would burn. I found out (laughs).

Smithsonian Institution

Keziah Dennis, George M. Cook's mother-in-law.

On Work

Russell Bradby: Ernest (Russell's brother) was a hustler. I got to give him that. At one time, he had three dump trucks. He made a lot of money with them trucks. He wasn't lazy, didn't have a lazy bone in his body. Jimmy (James Bradby Jr.), he would look for the easy way. Jimmy would go out and buy two beers and one cigar, and I'd come on the reservation and Jimmy's driving five miles an hour, drinking beer and smoking that cigar. Ernest was working for the state and had a water truck with a tank on back. When they

Ken Bradby Jr.

"Pipe of Joy" traditionally used at tribal council meetings. Chief and council members insert pipe stems and smoke at the start of the meeting. Made by Mary Bradby circa 1960.

blacktopped the roads, they had to keep them wet them all night. Drive all night, sprinkling it all night long. That was an easy job.

Daddy had quite a bit of land. Some had more than others. Albert Page had a lot of land. But some, like Peach Cook, he didn't have much land. When I was little, I was wishing we didn't have so much land 'cause when you got a little mule the plow makes a furrow about that big (holding his hands apart about eight inches, and laughs). Hard work.

Smthsonian Institution

James Bradby, Sr.

Joyce Bradby Krigsvold: I went to Richmond Tech and got my degree as a registered nurse. In Peach's last days, I took care of him. I felt bad because I knew it was embarrassing for him, but it didn't bother me. I was glad to do it. It was a great thing for me to be there and talk with him then, and to be there for him when he needed somebody. He would talk about the past if you got him going, but he didn't talk about those things much, and he didn't talk at all towards the end.

But his memory was still good. He knew who came to see him and who didn't. He would say, "When somebody was sick, I would go see them." He knew that there were those who didn't come to see him, and those who only came to see him once when he was sick. He didn't understand it. But I was so thankful that I was there when he passed away. I was grateful for that.

Joyce Bradby Krigsvold: One thing I'd like to point out. We had limited educational opportunities down here, but everybody did well. People worked for AT&T, Nabisco, all over. We did well despite the situations we faced.

Joyce Krigsvold

Grandma Dora Bradby in a Richmond studio.

On Race Relations

Russell Walter Ashby Plecker was the first registrar of Virginia's Bureau of Vital Statistics, serving from 1912 to 1946. For decades he spearheaded efforts to keep the white race pure in Virginia by forcing Indians and other non-whites to classify themselves as "colored."

Plecker was a staunch advocate of eugenics, a movement to preserve the integrity of white blood by preventing interracial breeding. He retired in 1946 at the age of 85 and died the following year.

Even in death and to this day, Plecker continues to frustrate the efforts of Virginia tribes to win federal recognition and thus collateral grants for housing, health care and education. One requirement is that a tribe prove continuous existence since 1900. Plecker, by purging Indians as a race, made that all but impossible.

Virginia Historical Society

Walter Plecker was the first registrar of Virginia's Vital Statistics.

Well into 2008, six Virginia tribes are seeking the permission of Congress to nullify this stipulation.

In 1943 Plecker sent a formal letter sent to state and local officials that captures the spirit and the mendacity of his eugenics crusade. It went to local voter registrars, physicians, health officers, nurses, school superintendents and clerks of court as a "Dear Co-worker" advisory. It may be the first official use of the term "these people" as code for his more explicit "these mongrels."

Excerpts follow, along with his detailed list of the known families who were "striving" to pass for white. The reader is immediately drawn to the New Kent list and can only wonder where the evidence lies, or why some families were mercifully excluded. The list included alternate spellings as well as cross references to other counties, most of which have been omitted here for clarity.

Smithsonian Institution

Thomas Langston, a preacher in the 19th century at Pamunkey Baptist.

Our December 1942 letter to local registrars set forth the determined effort to escape from the negro race groups of "free issues," or descendants of the "free mulattoes" prior to 1865 in

Family photo

**Rodessa Dennis at right, with her
mother and unidentified youngster.**

the United States census and various State records, as distinguished from slave negroes.

Now that these people are playing up the advantages gained by being permitted to give "Indian" as the race of the child's parents on birth certificates, we see the great mistake made in not stopping earlier the organized propagation of this racial falsehood. They have been using the advantage as an aid to intermarriage into the white race and to attend white schools, and they have been refusing to register with war draft boards as negroes. Three of these negroes from Caroline County were sentenced to prison for refusing to obey the draft law unless permitted to classify themselves as "Indians."

Some of these mongrels, finding that they have been able to sneak in their birth certificates as Indians are now making a rush to register as white. We find that a few local registrars have been permitting such certificates to pass through their hands unquestioned and without warning our office of the fraud. Those attempting this fraud should be warned that they are liable to a penalty of one year in the penitentiary.

Several clerks have likewise been actually granting them licenses to marry whites, or at least to marry amongst themselves as Indian or white. The danger of this error always confronts the clerk who does not inquire carefully as to the residence of the woman when he does not have positive information.

To aid all of you in determining just which are the mixed families, we have made a list of their surnames by counties and cities. This list should be preserved by all, even by those in

Family photo

Governor's tribute from the 1950s. Ernest Bradby is at far left and T.D. Cook at far right.

counties and cities not included, as these people are moving around over the State and changing race at the new place. A family has just been investigated which was always recorded as negro around Glade Springs, Washington County, but which changed to white and married as such in Roanoke County.

This is going on constantly and can be prevented only by care on the part of local registrars, clerks, doctors, health workers and school authorities. Please report all known or suspicious cases to the Bureau of Vital Statistics. All certificates of these people showing "Indian" or "white" are now being rejected and returned to the physician or midwife, but local registrars hereafter must not permit them to pass their hands uncorrected or unchallenged and without a note of warning to us.

Family photo

Chief Walter Bradby.

One hundred and fifty thousand other mulattoes in Virginia are watching eagerly the attempt of their pseudo-Indian brethren, ready to follow in a rush when the first have made a break in the dike.

Very truly yours,

W. A. Plecker, M.D.

State Registrar of Vital Statistics

Valentine Museum

Tecumseh Cook, known as Peach, dances at a governor's tribute during the 1960s.

Surnames of Virginia Families Striving

Albemarle: Moon, Powell, Kidd, Pumphrey.

Amherst: Adcock, Beverly (this family is now trying to evade the situation by adopting the name of Burch or Birch, which was the name of the white mother of the present adult generation), Branham, Duff, Floyd, Hamilton, Hartless, Hicks, Johns, Lawless, Nukles, Painter, Ramsey, Redcross, Roberts, Southwards, Sorrells, Terry, Tyree, Willis, Clark, Cash, Wood.

Bedford: McVey, Maxey, Branham, Burley.

Rockbridge: Cash, Clark, Coleman, Duff, Floyd, Hartless, Hicks, Mason, Mayse, Painters, Pultz, Ramsey, Southerds, Sorrell, Terry, Tyree, Wood, Johns.

Charles City: Collins, Dennis, Bradby, Howell, Langston, Stewart, Wynn, Custalow, Dungoe, Holmes, Miles, Page,

Allmond, Adams, Hawkes, Spurlock, Doggett.

New Kent: Collins, Bradby, Stewart, Wynn, Adkins, Langston.

Henrico and Richmond City: See Charles City, New Kent, and King William.

Caroline: Byrd, Fortune, Nelson.

Essex and King and Queen: Nelson, Fortune, Byrd, Cooper, Tate, Hammond, Brooks, Boughton, Prince, Mitchell, Robinson.

Elizabeth City & Newport News: Stewart (descendants of Charles City families).

Halifax: Epps, Stewart, Coleman, Johnson, Martin, Talley, Sheppard, Young.

Norfolk County & Portsmouth: Sawyer, Bass, Weaver, Locklear, King, Bright, Porter.

Westmoreland: Sorrells, Worlds, Atwells, Butridge, Okiff.

Valentine Museum

Chief Tecumseh Deerfoot Cook, at annual governor's tribute, 1960s.

Greene: Shifflett, Shiflet.
Prince William: Tyson, Segar.
Fauquier: Hoffman, Riley, Colvin, Phillips.
Lancaster: Dorsey.
Washington: Beverly, Barlow, Thomas, Hughes, Lethcoe, Worley.

Roanoke County: Beverly, Lee, Collins, Gibson, Moore, Goins, Ramsey, Delph, Bunch, Freeman, Mise, Barlow, Bolden, Mullins, Hawkins.

Scott: Dingus.

Russell: Keith, Castell, Stillwell, Meade, Proffitt.

Tazewell: Hammed, Duncan.

Wise: (See Lee, Scott, Smyth, and Russell counties.)

Virginia State Library

George M. Cook at 1901 governor's tribute. President William McKinley was there as well.

Louis Stewart: "Yeah, we had it tough. Everything was worse over here. But you know, Indians are funny. Ida Miles would say Indians were like flowers — all different colors. Now, the good colors, the "whites only" didn't bother you. But if I look dark, they might put a foot in my ass. And the white Indians, they wouldn't even bother them.

Let me tell you something. My daddy's brother, George Stewart, he used to come down here all the time 'til he married a white woman. Never came back, never bothered with my daddy or his own brother, all because they were married to Indian women. He had two daughters who worked at Phillip Morris, and whites only worked there, so he didn't want trouble for them. They threw out Tom Dennis, Willie Bradby, Irma and Richard. They all worked there and Richard was a boss there, but one fella got jealous of Richard and reported he had black blood in him too, so Richard got fired.

Virginia State Library

Annual Thanksgiving tribute shows unidentified child, Jimmy Bradby, Willis Allmond, Gov. Mills Goodwin, Daisy Bradby, Chief Tecumseh Cook.

"Me and Russell would run around a little bit. We'd go to dances, and get messed up, Claude Page was out there hittin' people. Claude was mean as (expletive). They used to hang around 17th & Market. They would take vegetables up there and sell 'em. Then they'd go in the bars. In them days, whites only, right? Well, one day Russell was hot, tired and not feelin' like puttin' up with foolishness. He went up there and the bartender wouldn't sell him a beer. Russell grabbed a beer and threw it right in his face."

Kevin Brown: "Ed was boarding with Tic (Ottigney Cook, George Major Cook's son) at Ida Miles' in Philly. Ida and Jim Miles had a house with Grampa, Tic, and I want to say Archie Collins but I'm not sure. They lived in kind of a bad part of town. Grampa was younger than Tic. When they took him out to a bar, it was the first time that Grampa ever drank. They were drinking and Grampa said they were up on the tables and war dancing and everything, whoopin' and hollerin'.

F.G. Speck

Ottigney Pontiac "Tic" Cook, son of George M. Cook.

When they were walking back, it was about 2 o'clock in the morning, and Tic was walking in the middle of the street. They were trying to get him on the sidewalk. Tic was loud, and Grampa said, "Tic! Be quiet! Quiet! You're gonna wake everybody up!" Tic stopped in the middle of the road and hollered at the top of his lungs (they were in a black part of town) "All you black son of a bitches, come on out here!" Lights were comin' on, people were lookin' out the windows, and he was whoopin' and hollerin' to fight. Grampa was scared to death. But they finally got Tic to calm down and go back to the boarding house where they stayed. But ol' Tic, he called the whole neighborhood out. Two in the morning."

In the South, a person was considered either white or colored. But colored included Negroes, Indians and Chinese. Mulattoes were mixed Caucasian and thus considered impure by Jim Crow standards.

The following testimony is taken from The Virginia Gazette in 1871 when the North Carolina Joint Senate and House Committee asked Robeson County Judge Giles Leitch about the "free persons of color" in his county.

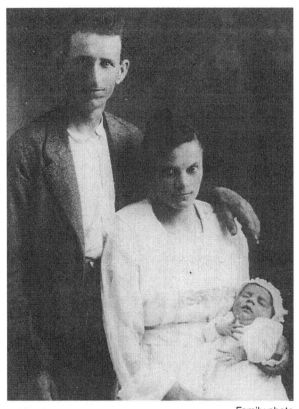

Family photo

Roy and Ada Bush, with baby. Ada was one of many Pamunkey women forced to leave the reservation after marrying a white man. She made pottery in her home in Roanoke and sold it on the reservation.

Senate: Half of the colored population?

Leitch: Yes sir, half of the colored population of Robeson County were never slaves at all.

Senate: What are they, Negroes?

Leitch: Well sir, I think they are a mixture of Spanish, Portuguese and Indian.

Senate: You think they are mixed Negroes and Indians?

Leitch: I do not think that in that class of population there is much Negro blood at all. I think they are of Indian origin.

Senate: I understand you to say that these seven or eight hundred persons that you designate as mulattoes are not generally Negroes?

Leitch: I do not think the Negro blood predominates.

Senate: the word 'mulatto' means a cross between the white and the Negro?

Family photo

Bernice Langston, my grandfather's sister.

Leitch: Yes sir.

Senate: You do not mean the word to be understood in that sense when applied to these people?

Leitch: I really do not know how to describe those people.

Being Native American didn't meet the standard of eligibility to vote. In 1829 John Marsh, a Pamunkey who served in the Revolutionary War and married a Catawba

Indian, filed suit in South Carolina for the right to vote. Judge C.J. Colcock issued the decree by a three-judge panel.

It is with regret I find myself obliged to declare, that by the laws of this State, the applicant is not intitled to a vote. He seems to be a man of excellent character, and has been useful to the country, both in a military and a civil capacity. But he belongs to a race of people who have always been considered as a separate and distinct class, never having been incorporated into the body politic. Whether the policy which led to this was wise is a question not for us to decide. Our ancestors thought it so, and all the laws of our State provide for the regulation of their affairs in a peculiar manner. When guilty of offences, they are tried by a particular tribunal, and in no respect are they considered as citizens. But above all, our constitution expressly confines the right of voting to free white men; and there can be no doubt that the term was used as contradistinguishing the white man from the Indian, and Negro, or mulatto.

Family photo

Ruth Cook, Peach's wife.

On Church

Joyce Bradby Krigsvold: What I remember about church on the reservation is that you didn't think about whether or you were going to go. You went to church on Sunday morning because it was something you did with the whole family. It was just something that the entire community did together.

In fact, most of the activities in the community were centered on the church. But the men and women wouldn't sit together. I can see right now in my mind where everybody sat — men on one side of the aisle, women on the other.

When they baptized someone, they would take them down by the river. They would change into the baptism clothes in one of the shanties, or

Bob Gray

Pamunkey Baptist Church was founded in 1865.

else at my mother's house by the river. The preacher would take them into the river and say some words over them as he baptized them. Then we'd have a community get together for the new church member. Nowadays we have that at the museum conference room.

Alexander Allmond, brother-in-law of Chief Terrill Bradby, and family. The large Bible reflected the influence of Christianity in Pamunkey society.

Russell Bradby: I had a good mom and dad, and we always went to church. My father was a good Christian man who taught Sunday school. He didn't smoke or chew nothin'. You couldn't even say "hell" around him. If my sisters Ruth and Bernice wanted to go dancing, he wouldn't want that.

Louis Stewart: When Peach's daddy (George Cook) died, I was a pallbearer at the funeral, behind the church there (pointing). You know, when we came up, we was big boys. Ain't no (expletive) about it. And I come up to be his pallbearer about 12 or 13 years old. Snow on the ground, cold. And they had one undertaker around, Shockley was his name. He had all the business here.

I used to live with Jimmy Bradby and his family for a while. His daddy was named Jim, too. He was the Sunday school teacher, so we all went to church.

T. D. Cook was a deacon of the church for over 40 years.

On Hunting & Fishing

Tecumseh Cook: When I started fishing, I could only paddle with one oar. Instead of two oars, I paddled with one oar and my daddy paddled on the other side to keep it straight.

You wouldn't want to believe this, but my mother used to knit these all the wintertime (holding up shad nets). These had to be knitted. Now we buy them already knitted, but I don't see how in the world anybody could knit one of these.

(Displaying needle used for altering nets so it can be

Smithsonian Institution

Deadfall trap at the river's edge.

Paul Miles checks his trap.

cast into the river), Now this needle I have in my hand, my daddy made it. This needle is probably a hundred years old, and I'm still using it. This other one's a paleface needle, this one is plastic, and my daddy's here is wood. He didn't pattern after the white man, the white man patterned after *him*. This was made long before the white man ever thought about one like this. We toss this one aside (throwing plastic needle behind him to the floor) and use the Indian one.

If you want to put the nets out just one time, you put out a tide gauge (sticking piece of branch in the river). When the tide's going out, the tide will be leaving that stick. You don't want to drift too far because you catch more shad when the net slacks up.

Shad are caught at slack water, as tide movement slows. When the tide is strong, the net is sweeping off the bottom. When the tide weakens, the net goes down some more until it gets down to the bottom of the river. We leave that stick there, and we watch it for a while. After a while, you see risin', and when it gets up to here (making a mark about two feet behind gauge), you know you got about three-quarters of an hour of tide runnin' yet, up the river.

You bait turtles with eels on hooks and line, tied to cane poles firmly placed in river floor. Try to catch eels about as big as your thumb and cut 'em up in pieces about an inch long. The turtles go wild over eels, it's the

Smithsonian Institution

John Dennis, George M. Cook's brother-in-law, displays otter skin.

best bait you can use. When you don't have eels you use catfish, but eels are much better. Many times, I've been out and filled a barrel (to store turtles on boat) up like that. Sometimes I caught more than I could get in the barrel.

Then you got to start tying them around in the boat.

A turtle has got all kinds of meat. I like the neck. Tastes more like chicken.

In the back of a deadfall trap, I put a stick down in case it moved from a high tide. I always put something in the back to keep it from moving. I put some bait in here, (pointing to one side) then some triggers here (beyond bait bowl), and the muskrat comes in here (points to front of trap).

This collar is made of wild grapevine. You place the collar here (front of the trap). Now (holding a five-foot pointed stick) this is called a sweepstick. You place the sweep-stick under the collar.

Smithsonian Institution

John Dennis demonstrates turkey call.

We use wild parsnip to connect the collar to the sweepstick. You push it in from this end here (near front of trap). You put a piece of bait on it, and block off the trap so he can come in only one way. When the twine on the noose breaks loose, it triggers the trap and the door slams down.

Louis Stewart: The pale faces, they liked sora huntin'. Sora is a good tastin' bird. For a sora horse, like a peach basket made of iron strips, you put wood in it and set it on a place in the flats on the river. Set fire to the wood in the sora horse to attract the sora, then you beat the sora down with a paddle. You got to push those boats with a pole to the flats. Liked to kill me.

[Author's note: It did kill "Sweet" Cook, (George Cook Jr.) my grandmother's brother. She told me, "He pushed his guts out."]

I did it once. People called down wantin' to hunt but they couldn't find nobody, so I did it. A few other guys were out with boatloads of palefaces, and they got their limit, but I didn't know much about doin' it. We only got a few. We was low boat.

Yeah, sora. They don't do that no more. They used to make a few dollars on that. I wouldn't go back out there if they paid me good money.

Smithsonian Institution

George Cook Jr. was known as "Sweet." He died as a result of pushing flatboats as a sora hunting guide. Grandma Dora, his sister, said he "pushed his guts out."

Russell Bradby: I remember when I used to catch muskrats, you know, trapping. Mr. Dickerson from up at Lester Manor didn't know nothing about muskrats. They

George M. Cook at work.

was selling brown muskrats then for one dollar and they was selling black ones for two. So I got an idea. I wet them, so that brown muskrats looked like blacks, and I sold them to him, and when the fur buyer came there to buy them from him, he said "I got a lot of black rats." So the buyer went through the bag, pulling them out and said, "I don't see no black rats." Mr. Dickerson shook his head and said 'That doggone Russell, he got me again!'

The following account of a Pamunkey turkey hunt is taken from "Indian Notes and Monographs: Chapters on the Ethnology of the Powhatan Tribes of Virginia," by Frank W. Speck, 1928.

A scene from the work of a day of a hunter conveys a picture of life at Pamunkey and an understanding of living conditions.

Unidentified Pamunkey hunter lies in wait.

A chilly northwest wind is blowing down the Pamunkey late in the afternoon when we leave the village and embark in Paul Miles' canoe, paddling toward the mouth of a sinuous lagoon called Great Creek. This flows out of the big swamp at the western end of the territory which the Pamunkey still call their own. Its fastnesses of swamp-gum, magnolia, and swamp-oak at high tide are flooded with the coffee-colored waters of the river.

At low tide, dropping two and three feet, the turbid waters leave a tangle of roots and hummocks of indescribable muddy congelation in tussocks eight or ten feet across. From the top of these rise clusters of gums, oaks and other trees. Some of their trunks tower 50 to 60 feet over the muddy floor of the swamp. In this memorable and gloomy vaulted fastness of malaria, the Pamunkey hunters have pursued the chase for centuries.

Paul Miles, who became chief after George Cook died in 1930, with shotgun. Young Peach is holding a goose.

Wild turkeys, the noblest of game birds, have survived generations of keen trappers along with ducks, bald eagles, geese, deer, raccoons, opossums, otter, mink and muskrat. Their ranks have been recruited from the flocks of birds and mammals which still make their migration through the Tidewater region. The great blue heron, the white young of the more Southerly herons, and the omnipresent great barred owl are the permanent denizens of these dank recesses.

When we leave the open river with its cheerful ripples lapping the sides of our canoe, we convert our paddles into poles and poke our way over mud bars into Great Creek. Each prod loosens a swirl of reddish mud which rises ever thicker through the opaque current. Now and then we send ahead in muddy ripples a fish that is startled by our advance into his roily domain. The smell of saturated mud, drenched dead wood and muddy leaves comes to us as the gas bubbles rise to the surface from our paddles.

As the tide is low, the whole floor of the swamp is carpeted in places with sodden sedge grass, while everywhere lie matted leaves coated with dried brown mud. Brown is the dominant color.

Smithsonian Institution

Paul Miles poses with Union Collins.

Brown are the tree trunks, marked distinctively to the high-tide level. Brown is the glazed mud and ooze, and glassy water in here where no wind strikes it.

Two or three bends of the lagoon carry us out of view of the river and the edge of the swamp. On all sides the drainways of the interior have cut through the floor, leading in slimy slopes to the edge of the water. Innumerable tracks of small animals are seen at each sluice. Here are muskrat, mink, otter and here and there one which the Pamunkey remarks in a whisper to be raccoon.

Finally, further in, are turkey.

The gun resting in the bow is now loaded and taken in hand ready for work as the guide, aroused to the importance of his task, plies his long oak paddle from the stern and forces the canoe over or around the mud bars and ooze shoals.

Smithsonian Institution

Paul Miles and Union Collins. Chief Miles was proficient at carving canoes out of tree trunks.

"Now if you see anything jump up, I want you to cut him down."

"I will," I whisper in reply.

Only the drip of a dozen drops from the evenly swaying pole-paddle announces our entrance into the solitude. How busy the Pamunkey huntsmen are in their swampy domain, when at every bend we see one of their deadfalls for mink, coon and otter, now soaked, mud-coated, and weed-clogged as they are exposed by the ebb tide.

"All right," I whisper again, as the steersman gives a shiver from his seat in the stern. It is the Pamunkey way of saying without words, "Watch closely, something moving!" A distant rustle of twigs on the right in a gum cluster is the first cause of alarm. I shiver once in my seat in response, and he turns the canoe with a silent shove to the right so as to throw me about facing the noise.

Smithsonian Institution

Aside from the meat, turkeys also provided feathers for regalia.

What will it prove to be, a deer aroused? Or will a turkey burst away? A furtive rustle, a noisy flutter, and a white-throated sparrow pops into view with a piquant air. It flutters loudly enough to disturb the silence of the swamp, and we resume our stealthy passage into another arm whose slimy banks rise several feet on both sides.

Here the creek is barely 15 feet wide. On both sides are the ski-'tonos, the "red berries" in the Pamunkey dialect, upon which the turkeys feed. All the water-gums are showing small isolated berries. These like-wise furnish food for the turkeys. While the Pamunkeys may have forgotten their native tongue, it is not surprising to find that in their nat-ural history and hunting vocabulary some last Indian words survive.

Another shiver from the steersman warns me again of game detected. At the same instant a form moves on the horizontal branch of a monster gum-tree whose roots form a vault of mud-coated columns leading to its massive buttress.

"Let him have it!" No, it is only the spirit of the swamp,

Smithsonian Institution

Chief Miles was tried in the drowning death of a young girl and was cleared.

The modern Pamunkey shad hatchery has been in operation since 1918. From the late 1800s to the early 1900s, shad was the most economically valuable fish harvested for food in Maryland and Virginia.

the barred-owl, which now turns his ogreish head about and drops off to another rampike in noiseless flight.

Five minutes later we hear his vacant "whoo-oo" farther off and an answer from his mate, still more filmy and remote. The sound is indeed fitting to the exotic atmosphere of the swamp. As it is nearing sundown, we look for a motionless pool to stop and listen, to harken for the roosting calls of the hens or possibly hear the rush of wings as the great birds fly to roost on some limb 50 feet above. They will crane their necks in all directions before contracting their great bodies to the smallest compass to simulate the knots on gums, and tuck their heads under wings to sleep like any secure barnyard fowl. This is the critical time. Every sharpened sense of both hunters and turkeys is keyed to action.

"There goes one!" A whisper and a powerful shiver convey the observation. Too far away. He has bolted for some inaccessible thicket and we see no more of him.

Now we wait 20 minutes in our position while the Indian holds the canoe still by poking his pole-paddle into several feet of submarine mud. There is not a sound. Three or four birds fly high, probably woodpeckers. A distant hound's yelping proclaims another Indian somewhere on the move.

It is now time to turn back, as darkness sets in heavily with a penetrating damp that will defy the strenuous paddling necessary when we emerge again upon the open river. The canoe is swung around and the Indian poles her

Family photo

Peach minding his traps.

swiftly but silently along. The evening gleam on the horizon shows we are nearing the edge of the swamp. We tarry and enter yet another draw to examine the high tree tops for birds roosted there, for at this darkening half-hour the birds are all off the ground. Several suspicious clumps turn out to be only knots, or gnarled lightning-blasted branches, or clusters of dense mistletoe.

Back to the river again, as the game is over for tonight. A crescent moon above the evening star is framed by bulky cloud masses. The wind has lulled, and we make for the landing beach on the reservation shore where for generations Pamunkey hunters have likewise drawn up their canoes after engaging in the same perform-ance we have just been through.

Family photo

Frank Bradby, the author's brother, resides in the house of their grandparents and runs Lay Landing Farm on the premises.

On Lester Manor

Lester Manor is an estate near the entrance of the Pamunkey reservation. Richard McCluney of Williamsburg grew up there. His grandparents, Maurice and Maggie Dickinson, ran a store and the post office, which became a social hub. Maggie became a revered teacher, but not before a rocky start.

Richard McCluney: My grandmother came to teach on the Pamunkey reservation. Her first teaching job was supposed to be in the town of Achilles in Gloucester County. She had never met the superintendent but was recommended by her professors and the president of her college to a minister who knew the superintendent.

Tidewater Review

Lester Manor lies outside the reservation.

George M. Cook with daughter Pocahontas and wife Theodora.

In those days, there was no public transportation to Gloucester. My grandmother went by train from Richmond to Williamsburg. She hired a mule wagon and driver to take her to Yorktown. It was late summer or early fall. School should have already started, but the teacher had gotten sick.

It was a very stormy day and they didn't get to Yorktown until nearly dark. The York River was rough with whitecaps, and the wind was blowing with brief squalls of rain. The wagon driver unloaded my grandmother and her trunk on the beach and stuck a pole with a flag in the sand, and then drove off. He said someone would see the flag and come for her.

She sat on the beach in the rain and wind for a long time. Finally she saw a boat coming across the river. A man in a rowboat about the size of a small fishing boat arrived. He told her the superintendent was expecting her. He loaded her and the trunk into his boat.

She had never seen a body of water as big as the river at Yorktown. By the time they started across, it was evening and the storm had gotten so dark that you couldn't see the other side. She thought she was crossing an ocean — in a rowboat!

Finally they could see some light on the shore. When they got ashore a carriage and driver were waiting for them. The carriage had been sent by the superintendent. They were off into the stormy night.

Smithsonian Institution

Bernice Bradby Langston was a student of Maggie Dickinson's.

I don't know how long it took, but she recalled it was a long time. Sometime in the evening she arrived at the superintendent's house. His wife had saved dinner for my grandmother and something hot to drink after she changed into dry clothes.

As she sat down the eat, the superintendent said how much he appreciated her coming to help with the school on such short notice. But unfortunately, he didn't have a job for her after all. An epidemic of diphtheria had broken out and he had to close all the schools. He didn't know when they would reopen.

So the next day, she reversed the trip. The weather was a little better, but I don't think he even offered to pay her transportation. Her first teaching assignment wasn't, and she went back home.

I remember stories about the cannery, which I think was falling down and over-grown when I was very young. It was located three-quarters of mile up the road from Lester Manor. That was near and behind Mr. Dunn's store.

Smithsonian Institution

Union Collins and Pocahontas Cook.

It was a big operation at the time, as I remember hearing my grandparents talk about it. It employed lots of folks during the canning season.

Amazingly, there were in this sparsely populated rural area four stores within three miles. There was my grandfather's store at Lester Manor and also the Lester Manor Post Office. A mile up the road was Dunn's store. A half-mile farther was Mike's store, which was owned by Mike Previs. He was one of several brothers who emigrated from Poland. A mile-and-half farther was Lanesville store, which was another post office. Then about a mile further was another store.

My grandfather's store and the post office did not sell beer or wine, but customers came because of the post office. It was the biggest store with the most stuff, and he liked everyone and gave them credit. He also sold Esso gas. Mr. Dunn had a pretty good-sized store but only about half as big as Lester Manor. He had beer and ice cream.

Mike's store was pretty small and didn't have a lot, but it had a little bit of basic things. He sold a lot of beer. Lanesville was tiny and didn't have hardly anything except the Post Office and bread and eggs. The next store was big, two-story. The owners lived upstairs. The main store didn't have a whole lot of merchandise, but they had a few booths and some stacks and they had ice cream and beer and music. Competition in the free market!

Smithsonian Institution

George M Cook. Lester Manor is where the train stopped nearest the reservation.

There were a lot of snakes at the Lester Manor Club, down by the water and around the warehouse and boathouse especially. James Lambert Bradby used to keep a shotgun down there in the small corner room where the working outboards and oars lived or in the main warehouse, I don't remember. He would reach in the door, grab the shotgun, and BLAM! blow away some snake on the dock. I think these were cottonmouths primarily.

There were a lot of snakes. The black ones I think he tolerated because they helped keep the poisonous ones away, but don't know that for sure. Over time I saw black, blue, rat, copperhead, cottonmouth and an assortment of unknown water snakes. I don't know if all were moccasins or harmless. I never did learn all the different kinds. Never did see a rattler.

I finally got comfortable with black snakes and garter snakes and little green snakes. I would pick those up and sometimes take one home. But after being told,

Smithsonian Institution

Grandma Dora in a pensive mood.

"Don't bring that snake up to the house!" I mostly just watched them.

The "warehouse" down the hill from Joyce's house was the manager's house, located on the riverside from a larger house that I thought of as the Manor House. There was a

Chief Cook and his son Major, who after serving in World War I came home and mysteriously committed suicide at the family home.

newer, one-story house that I think was called "the club-house" where the Vanderpools stayed during their visit. Dora would give us food in the kitchen, but we would watch TV in the living room in the manager's house.

I remember Kenneth Bradby had a room where he had all of his electronics and ham radio gear. I remember his old car. It needed a lot of work, but I thought it was wonderful. Dora's story triggered the memory of the old great car that always stayed in the warehouse except when the Vanderpools or guests were coming.

The warehouse was a wonderful and scary place. Not only did the car live there, that's where Jimmy Bradby kept

Chief Cook after a fruitful fishing expedition.

tools and parts to fix the car, the lawnmowers, and most of the outboard engines. Some of them were always being worked on. Joyce may have been permitted to touch the tools, but I was not since they were off-limits to both of us. We weren't supposed to go in there except when her dad was working and had the building open.

The great caution was not to go in without Jimmy because of snakes. It was not uncommon to find a big black snake on the dock, in the drive, in the warehouse. More often, one would find complete snake skins in the warehouse on boxes, barrels, great blocks and coils of rope. It was a magic place. Kenneth's old Ford was open and sat in the yard down by the warehouse. It was pretty rusty and weeds had grown up around it, which made it a good place for snakes. Sure enough, there were snake skins in there on the floor and just visible behind the seat. There may have been snakes that liked to curl up in there. Or just putting skins in there may have been a sure way Kenneth or Jimmy had of keeping Joyce, me and especially any strangers out of Kenneth's car while he was away.

My personal fear was spiders. There were quite a few black widows around Lester Manor and an inordinate number around the warehouse. Why, in my childhood, I must have seen at least *two* there! So maybe my fear was unfounded, but they were *big ones*!

Theophilus Dennis, brother-in-law of George M. Cook, served as interim chief in 1900.

I remember one of the Indian men who had an outhouse. Lots of folks did in those days. I figured Joyce and I were real lucky since both of us lived in places with indoor toilets and running water. Anyway, an Indian man, so the story went, got bitten by a black widow in the outhouse and on his "privates" as my Grandfather would say. The story goes that it swelled up and turned dark and nearly killed him with pain, if not with the actual poison.

I was about four or five years old when I heard that, and I've been afraid of spiders ever since. As a result, I never

George M. Cook is seated on right with his daughter Captola beside him. Terrill Bradby is fourth from left.

liked visiting my uncle's farm because they only had an outhouse — with spiders in it. Scared me to death to go down there, especially at night because there were no lights and you couldn't see where the spiders were.

Tidewater Review newspaper: In the late 1800s and early 1900s, Lester Manor was a booming railway town. A key connection between King William, King & Queen and the big city of Richmond, travelers, salesmen and merchandise made many a journey upon the tracks that still stand today.

Just a teenager of 18, Bob Walsh remembers the first time he came to Lester Manor's train depot, in 1948. "It was a great time with some great memories," he said. "It was a good part of my life, and it influenced me a great deal." Walsh went on to work for the Southern Railway Co. as a telegraph operator until 1955.

Lester Manor Depot, or train station, was built in 1859. Around the same time, several other buildings were constructed, including the Lester Manor Hotel & Tavern and the Lester Manor General Store and Post Office. The original buildings have long since disappeared, but thanks to the historical nostalgia of Walkerton native Carroll Lee Walker, new representations stand in their place today.

Family photo

Maurice Dickinson with his grandson Richard McCluney, 1948.

"Lester Manor was a thriving little town at one time when the railroad was started," Walker said. "When I was 10 years old, I used to go there to get coal to bring back to Walkerton to run the cannery."

In its heyday, the railway was a huge economic boost for the area. Its roots can be traced back to 1856 when Alexander Dudley of King & Queen chartered the Richmond & York River Railroad with several other prominent businessmen. The line ran from Richmond to West Point.

After the construction of Lester Manor's depot, a stagecoach service owned by Ben Walker began running to King William Court House and Walkerton. The service delivered mail and could hold up to eight passengers. When the hotel and tavern was built, it served stage passengers and traveling salesmen on their rounds to their rural customers.

Although the buildings Walker had constructed are not exact replicas, they are idyllic representations.

"The store had everything in it – groceries,

Family photo

Train station as it appeared in 1950.

eggs, drinks, candy. "It was just your regular country store," said Grover Miles, who grew up on the neighboring Pamunkey Indian reservation. "

Miles, 77, remembers walking to the store as a child to get tobacco for his father and groceries and the mail for his mother. "The old country store had everything from materials to sewing thread to fertilizers and groceries. It always had a great big wheel of aged cheddar cheese."

Walsh said he learned many life lessons in Mr. Dickinson's store where most of the men would gather and share stories. "It was real colorful," he said diplomatically.

"It was just a place in the community for people to sit and talk and catch up"

Eventually the stagecoach transitioned into the Bristow Bus Line, and the country store installed gas pumps. Then the railway stopped carrying passengers and only delivered freight.

Walsh used to receive at least one telegram a day that required he call the recipient or track down a neighbor. Sometimes he would use a pole with a wire in the middle and the train would simply grab the message as it went by him. "I'm standing two feet from the train," he recalled. "It

Francis Hubbard, Tidewater Review

Depot restoration was done by 2008.

would be the same for me. He'd stick his message on a wire and I'd get it as he went through."

Walsh has never forgotten the people or the lessons he learned at Lester Manor. Mr. Dickinson used to always tell him, "Keep your foot on the rock. You'll be a good boy."

Pamunkey Chief Tecumseh Deerfoot Cook was a frequenter of the country store, telling many stories. He even taught Walsh how to hunt. Walsh recalled that he had long black hair and his native call could be heard a mile away.

— **Frances Hubbard, May 2008**

On the Civil War

Ever since Jamestown, Native Americans have been treated poorly. Under the President Andrew Jackson in the 1830s, the government all but designated them as second-class citizens. For a time, Pamunkey braves were stripped of their weapons, removing their main means of survival: hunting.

Prejudice was strikingly evident in the Southeast, where Indians and blacks were considered genetically inferior to whites.

Aboriginal resentment during the Civil War grew strong, and nowhere was that more evident than at the

Library of Congress

Union troops over-ran the reservation in May 1862.

Pamunkey reservation, then referred to by some as "Indiantown."

Massive Union troop movement into the area caused a Confederate retreat. White House, an estate near Pamunkey famous as Martha Custis's residence prior to her marrying George Washington, was overtaken by Union troops, and the local railroad became their supply line.

Gen. George McClellan made use of several Pamunkey men as land and river guides, essentially as scouts or spies. However, the local Collosse Baptist Church, which counted whites as well as Pamunkeys in the congregation, no longer welcomed those who fought on the Union side.

One man, Terrill Bradby, who would one day become chief of the Pamunkeys, served the Union cause on

Library of Congress

White House, home of widow Martha Custis, was commandeered by Union troops.

land and on ships as a guide and, eventually as a spy. He reported on Confederate encampment positions under the employ of Pinkerton's Secret Service. While onboard a ship in the James River, he was wounded in the leg by

Causeway across the Pamunkey where Confederate soldiers walked the men of Pamunkey to a train and face trial in Richmond as Union Army sympathizers.

Confederate shrapnel, which plagued him the rest of his life.

He was among a group of Pamunkeys taken to Richmond for treason to the Confederacy. Before he boarded the train, he kicked up his leg, feigned losing his shoe and went to the woodline to fetch it. From there, he took off running and stopped long enough to cover himself with leaves. Years later he recalled vividly that he could hear the soldiers as they searched for him. In Richmond, the Pamunkeys were eventually acquitted.

Later Terrill worked for the Smithsonian Institution in an effort to promote the Pamunkey people to the rest of the world. In 1893 he was an emissary to the Chicago Exposition, where he tried to convince other Native Americans to join the Pamunkeys in an effort to keep the blood lines purely aboriginal, if not exclusively Pamunkey. He was chief of the Pamunkeys around 1902.

His notes are difficult to read but were deciphered by James Mooney of the Smithsonian. He was accused at some point in his service with the Army of the Potomac of causing the death of his brother, Sterling Bradby, a river guide for the Union forces and one-time chief of the Pamunkeys. Details have been lost as to court records, but Laurence M. Hauptmann reported in his book "Between Two Fires" that Mooney recorded Gen. Ulysses Grant as the presiding judge.

Richmond Dispatch, Aug. 1, 1862:

Information having been sent to this city that the Federal army, while operating on the Chickahominy, was piloted and sided by the Pamunkey Indians, detective officer George W. Thomas was dispatched last week to King William County, with a squad of men, for the purpose of arresting such of the mongrel tribe as were engaged in the business. The party

Richmond Dispatch

The prison the Pamunkey men were held at in Richmond was called Castle Thunder, a modified tobacco warehouse.

entered the village on Friday night, and captured eleven, one of whom escaped on the way back, and three more were discharged after an examination at King William Court-House, while the remaining six were brought on to Richmond, where they are now held as prisoners. We understand that they acknowledge the charge alleged against them, but urge as an excuse that they were forced into the Federal service. Two citizens of King William, named Lipscomb, charged with holding intercourse with the enemy, were arrested and brought up at the same time. Some difficulties were experienced by the party on the route.

On arriving near the White House they found Colonel Thornton's pickets driven in by the enemy, who came up the Pamunkey river in batteaux, but were turned back before they had an opportunity of committing any depredations. This rendered a change in the original plan necessary, and the squad was obliged to proceed with much caution, though the object was successfully accomplished, as we have stated. No Yankees have made their appearance at the White House since the day to which we have alluded.

Richmond Dispatch

Another photo of Castle Thunder prison in Richmond.

On "Peach"

In the winter of 1899, Theodora Cook, wife of Chief George Cook, gave birth to the fifth of eight children. Tecumseh Deerfoot Cook was born in their home on the Pamunkey reservation. Named for two characters in a Pocahontas play staged by the Pamunkeys in the 19th century, young Tecumseh learned hunting, fishing and trapping from his father early on.

He received the nickname "Peach" at his mother's knee when she once exclaimed, "Come give me a peach!" It was her word for a kiss. Eventually she would just look at him and say "Peach!" and he would run up to kiss her cheek. Others picked up on this endearment, and the nickname remained with him for all his 103 years.

Family photo

Tecumseh Deerfoot Cook, chief of Pamunkey 1942-84.

He received the totality of his eighth-grade education in

the one-room schoolhouse on the reservation. He used to accompany his father on trips to the governor's mansion in Richmond to pay the annual tribute of wild game. It was a tradition kept since the 1677 treaty with the white settlers, which declared:

"That every Indian King and Queen in the month of March every yeare with some of theire great men tender their obedience to the R't Honourable his Majesties Govern'r at the place of his residence, wherever it shall be, and then and there pay the accustomed rent of twentie beaver skinns, to the Govern'r and alsoe their quit rent aforesaid, in acknowledgment that they hold their Crownes, and Lands of the great King of England."

This evolved into the present-day Thanksgiving tribute. Peach vividly recalled these occasions.

Family photo

Young Peach posing for a Richmond portrait photographer.

"There were many, many trips. Most times we took a deer. Other times we'd take fish or beaver hides. I can't remember missing [a tribute] but about twice in all my life. We had to take the deer up there on the train. The passenger train ran from Richmond to West Point. We'd walk from Main Street Station carrying a long pole with a deer on it, two men walking down the street. We were taking everybody's eyes walking to the governor's mansion from the train station."

He married Ruth Bradby in 1925. Jim Crow laws made gainful employment for Indians in Virginia nearly impossible. Enticed by the promise of jobs "up North," Peach and Ruth left the Pamunkey for Pennsylvania. They were hired by the Campbell Soup Co. in Philadelphia and eventually worked there nearly two decades.

Family photo

G. Warren Cook, Peach's son, was vice chief into 2008.

Then the couple returned home. As Peach recalled, "They elected me chief in 1942 and I served until 1984. The night of the election, they gave everyone a grain of corn and a pea, and passed the hat around." A grain of corn placed in the hat was a yea vote, a pea was a nay. Every four years, a new election took place, and Peach continued as chief for the next four decades.

During the 1940s and 1950s, life for Indians improved in several ways. The federal Office of Indian Affairs declared that all American Indians had the right to vote in 1948. In 1954 the Virginia General Assembly set the definitive standard of tribal Indian status with great precision: "Members of Indian tribes in this Commonwealth having one-fourth or more of Indian blood and less than one-sixteenth of Negro blood shall be deemed tribal Indians."

Family photo

Peach with his brother Ottigney Cook's granddaughter Debbie and sons.

In 1975 Peach asked the Native American Rights Fund to intervene on the Pamunkeys' behalf in a suit against the Southern Railway Co. More than 22 acres of reservation land that had been taken by the company's predecessors in 1855. The railroad settled in 1979 for $100,000. That same year, the Pamunkey Indian Museum first opened its doors.

Peach retired in 1984 when his wife of 59 years was

diagnosed with Alzheimer's disease. He chose to care for Ruth personally instead of placing her in a home. She passed in 1989.

Peach spent his remaining years participating in various projects, including an educational documentary, Thanksgiving tributes, and as a speaker at functions. He also served as an active member in his beloved Pamunkey Baptist Church.

On his 100th birthday, a grand celebration was held on the grounds of the museum. Television cameras and newspaper reporters captured the event as Peach stood up and deftly performed a ceremonial dance step as tom-toms kept in time. When asked the secret of a long life, he said, with a twinkle in his eye, "Eat plenty of raccoons and muskrats and drink Pamunkey River water." He added, "But lay off the possum."

Uncle Peach passed away April 13, 2003. Some 150 people lined the inside of the church. At least that many

Peach's siblings Captola, Ottigney and Pocahontas.

stood respectfully outside. When the preacher asked if anyone had anything to say about the man, one after another spoke of their memories of him. Some were tearful, some in fond remembrance, and all were with a sense that God had bestowed on them a great honor. They all had known the man they called Peach.

Janet Fast

Peach in headdress.

On George Major Cook

George Major Cook was chief of the Pamunkeys from 1902 until his death in 1930. He told his daughter Captola that his father Major drowned in the Pamunkey River and was found when his long black hair was spotted floating in the water. His mother Caroline raised George Major. He married Theodora Octavia Dennis and had eight children, one of whom died before reaching maturity.

He was an outspoken proponent for his people's rights and ethical treatment. Here is a speech he gave in 1928 in two parts. The first appears scripted and the second more extemporaneous.

Smithsonian Institution

Chief George Major Cook.

How! Heap big day, paleface. I am the great Wahunsunacoke, chief of the noble Pamunkeys, the last existing remnant of that dominant confederacy over which our great sachem Powhatan ruled. History and tradition furnishes conclusive proof that we are the lineal descendants of the original Pamunkey, the most formidable tribe of that great werowance Powhatan's confederacy, who met the first Virginia colonists here in America. We boast that we are the lineal descendants of the original actors of that world renowned drama: the capture of Captain John Smith by Opechancanough, the trial by King Powhatan, and her rescue by little Snow Feather who was better known as Pocahontas.

Family photo

George Cook posing for a Chesterfield cigarette ad.

Not only 300 years ago in colonial times, but today, on the banks of the Pamunkey, 24 miles east of that old historic capital, while many of our brother red men have been driven to the land of the sitting sun, while many of our bones lie bleached beneath the Arctic and Antarctic skies, we own and occupy that God-given spot your forefathers founded.

That is why in the beautiful springtime we can gather flowers in May, and scatter them over mounds over our ancestors. There we sing our green corn dances. There we sing our peace dances. There we tell our squaws and papooses of the happy days that are gone by. Not only of the days that are gone by, but of the days that soon will come. That of King Powhatan, Opechancanough, Chatnohakop, Totopotomoy, Chanco, Opitchipan, Nanticoke, Little Snow Feather and all the braves that have gone before. We will paddle our canoes across that river of life, and be there proud on that evergreen shore. Nano-noyeeyeeyee! We gather not only to smoke the pipe of peace, but to gather our red brothers and palefaces to smoke the pipe in peace, chasing the pronged deer, and sitting down in peace under the shade of trees, in our happy, happy hunting ground. Yip! Yeeheehee! Wahoo!

Chief Cook in regalia.

Part 2

How, paleface, heap big day. You ask me about Pamunkey's tribute to the governor of Virginia. We made a treaty with the government in colonial days and we renewed it with the General Assembly of Virginia, whereby the Pamunkeys should occupy their reservation, so long as the Pamunkey River ebbed and flowed. Our parts of the treaty, we have never broken. But the palefaces, I am sorry to say, have broken their treaty so much that we don't even know where the peace is. We carried a tribute from Governor Spottswood to the present Governor Byrd. We have not broken our custom until today. I myself have had the honor of taking the choicest game, the choicest fish, the choicest deer that the Pamunkey can afford to each governor, from Governor Cameron to the present governor. We are preparing now to take to Governor Byrd the choicest buck that can be found. The largest-pronged deer that Pamunkey can afford, we are preparing to take to him. And I hope that for many successive years to come, that Pamunkeys shall keep their treaty, even though the palefaces have broken theirs.

Smithsonian Institution

Chief Cook at home.
Peach at left in background.

On Recent Times

Russell Bradby: I got real sick about three years ago. They didn't think I'd make it. They had my daughter so sure I wouldn't make it that she got upset and sold a lot of my clothes and started thinking about funeral arrangements. But I came back, started eating better, and got better. I looked around and asked her, "Where's my blue suit?" She sold seven suits!

I wouldn't want to go back now. I got all my friends here now. I left there (the reservation) when I was 24 years old. Haven't lived there since. I went to school there 'til the seventh grade. Went into the Army, retired from the Army, retired from Civil Service, retired from the Sheriff's Department. So I did pretty good for an under-educated kid.

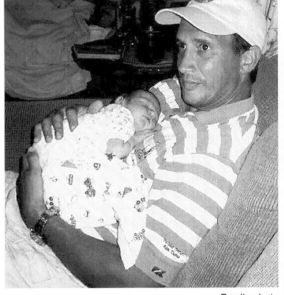

Family photo

Frank Bradby of Lay Landing Farm, home of his great grandfather James E. Bradby, holds his cousin River Cook, great grandson of Tecumseh "Peach" Cook.

Stewart Bradby: I was drivin' until a while ago. I was driving and I ended up in the cornfield. My son said he didn't want me drivin' no more.

Kevin Brown: Tic came back to the res, but I don't know if it was for a homecoming or a funeral. They were all standin' on a pier, and somebody said, "Tic, I remember you used to swim across the river when you were a young man." And now Tic was about seventy. He took his coat off and said "Hold my coat, boy!" Tic took off his shoes and jumped in, still wearin' his dress shirt and dress pants. He swam across the river, touched the other side, waved and swam back. Seventy years old.

Family photo

Kevin Krigsvold, son of Joyce Bradby Krigsvold, with daughter Sabine, wife Sasha and her mother Fran. Kevin won an Emmy for his work as a NASA producer of television programming.

On Pocahontas

Here's a comparison of 17th century Pocahontas narratives and a play by "Powhatan's Pamunkey Indian Braves."

The debate over the veracity of the "rescue" of Capt. John Smith at the hands of Pocahontas (real name Matoaka), daughter of Powhatan (Wahunsunacoke), has raged for centuries. Smith's own account recalls:

...Two great stones were brought before Powhatan: then as many as could laid hands on him, dragged him to them, and thereon laid his head, and being ready with their clubs, to beate out his braines, Pocahontas the King's dearest daughter, when no intreaty could prevaile, got his head in her armes, and laid her owne upon his to save him from death: whereat the

Family photo

Gov. Miles is at the far left posing with the Pocahontas players in Jamestown, 1907.

Pocahontas players, 1899.

Emperour was contented he should live to make him hatchets, and her bells, beads, and copper...

Moses Coit Tyler (A History of American Literature; 1879) states:

But the energetic Captain had an eager passion for making tours of exploration along the coast and up the rivers; and after telling how he procured corn from the Indians and thus supplied the instant necessities of the starving colonists, he proceeds to relate the history of a tour of discovery made by him up the Chickahominy, on which tour happened the famous incident of his falling into captivity among the Indians. The reader will not fail to notice that in this earliest book of his, written before Powhatan's daughter, the princess Pocahontas, had become celebrated in England, and before Captain Smith had that enticing motive for representing himself as specially favored by her, he speaks of Powhatan as full of friendliness to him; he expressly states that his own life was in no danger at the hands of that Indian potentate; and of course he has no sit-

Pocahontas play, 1907.

uation on which to hang the romantic incident of his rescue by Pocahontas from impending death.

Margaret Huber of the University of Mary Washington's Anthropology Department believes we tend to give Pocahontas credit for emotions and a response that makes sense to us, and then we make the circumstances fit.

It is important to remember that Powhatan was a decisive leader and not weak-minded. Smith was a serious rival. And Powhatan was not the kind to have policy decided by the whim of a child – even a favorite one.

Perhaps the earliest photo of the Pocohantas Players,1881. Theodora Dennis is standing third from left. Her future husband is 21-year-old George Major Cook, standing second from right.

Huber's bottom line on the famous rescue: "It was a put-up job," she said. Her theory is that the event was staged with Powhatan's approval and blessing. Powhatan wanted Smith to think that it was only because of his generosity that the Englishman was allowed to live. "I believe Pocahontas was acting for Powhatan and not on an impulse of her own," Huber said. "They went through the motion of killing him and then they made him a brother. I think Pocahontas' feelings for him would have been a sister's love – sisterly affection." Christian F. Feest (The Powhatan Tribes," pages 41-42), among others, support this theory. Accounts of other "spontaneous" ritualistic performances abound in early histories (Beverley, Book 3, p. 35, etc.).

In the end, according to Edwin Slosson ("What There Is at the Jamestown Exposition." The Independent,11 July, 73–81. 1907):

It does not make a particle of difference whether relics are authentic or not. Those who are susceptible to such telluric currents get the same thrill when they stand on the erroneously identified site of an imaginary event as they do on the real spot where something did happen. The history of hagiography proves that pseudo-saints work just as many miracles as true ones. Tho the bones of a martyr multiply like the loaves and fishes they never lose their power. No doubt the same holds true for patriotic relics. It is to be hoped so.

While such ideological meanderings may satisfy the unaffected masses, when the loss of cultural identity threatens the very existence of a segment of the population, we all as human beings instinctively take measures to ensure survival. After the Nat Turner Rebellion in 1831, new laws meant to ensure that such incidents would not be repeated affected not only slaves, but free Negroes and mulattoes as well. Tidewater Indians were required to legal-

NOTICE!

POWHATAN'S
PAMUNKEY INDIAN BRAVES
—WILL PERFORM AT—

on_____1898,

IN THE FOLLOWING INDIAN ROLES AND COSTUMES:
Green Corn Dance, Pamunkey Indian Marriage, Snake Dance by Deerfoot, War Dance, Capture of Capt. John Smith and the saving of his life by Pocahontas.

The Above will be Performed by

W. T. BRADBY	POWHATAN
HOWARDLEE ALLMOND	POCAHONTAS
T. W. LANGSTON	CAPT. JOHN SMITH
T. S. DENNIS	OPECHANCANOUGH
BILL BRADBY	MEDICINE MAN
JOHN DENNIS	SATNOHACO
EVANS BRADBY	DEERFOOT
T. T. DENNIS	TECUMSEH
G. M. COOKE	CAYATANIT
E. R. ALLMOND (Assistant Manager)	BIG DIVER

Admission_____ Children_____

Smithsonian Institution

Posted advertisement for Pocahontas play, 1898.

ly prove their heritage, a task made more difficult due to a combination of general illiteracy among the various tribes and the fact that state records of marriages and births were chaotic (when in existence at all). In 1845, a historian wrote of the Pamunkey Indians, "Their Indian character is nearly extinct, by intermixing with whites and Negroes." Ten years later, an anonymous visitor claimed the reservation to be inhabited "by the most curious intermixture of every class and color." (Feest, 1990, p.73)

These rumors were perpetuated by white neighbors of the Pamunkeys, as it provided grounds to petition the Virginia Assembly in 1843, claiming inhabitants of the reservation "would be deemed and taken to be free mulattoes, in any Court of Justice; as it is believed they all have one fourth or more of negro blood." As such, the residents had no right to live there; they should be removed and the land sold. The Pamunkey submitted their own petition for

Smithsonian Institution

Captola Cook Miles, daughter of Chief George Major Cook, played Pocahontas in the play as a child.

mercy, stating "There are many here who are more than half-blooded Indians, tho we regret to say there are some here who are not of our tribe."

The assembly rejected the petition to displace the Pamunkeys, but a lesson was learned. Their very survival as a people was contingent on being "seen" as Indians. In other words, we needed to be Indians in the eyes of others, as well as ourselves. And to be as inconspicuous as possible.

By the Civil War, the Pamunkeys had all but disappeared, in the minds of most. They were not taxed on the reservation, so they did not appear on official records. They continued hunting, fishing, and began farming at an increasing rate. In an effort to keep their "Indianness" in the public consciousness, in about 1880 the Pamunkey began to perform a stage version of the rescue of Capt. John Smith by Pocahontas, if only to remind white Virginians of the debt they owed to the maiden who saved

Smithsonian Institution

T. D. Cook was named for two characters in the play, Tecumseh and Deerfoot.

Jamestown and subsequently Virginia, and to remind them her people remain among them. As the sparse dress of 1607 Powhatan Indians would not be acceptable in the era, fringed buckskins and beads were worn by the actors. A playbill of the day is shown below.

Perhaps the most publicized performance occurred in 1907, at the Jamestown Exposition. An observer noted:

As is always the case, visitors to the Jamestown Exposition encountered representations of Indians through their prior conceptions, which would have included the idea of the "disappearing" Indian, reinforced by the recent ending of the major Indian wars of the West. While living Native people were present and active at the exposition, they were representing events and ways of life from the past, and visitors had a certain flexibility in how they could interpret those representations. Many undoubtedly simply saw them as relics of that past, representing (with some greater or lesser degree of authenticity) vanished or vanishing peoples, events, and ways of life.

Family photo
Young Pocahontas Cook.

The Pamunkey performed the play for more than 30 years, usually on the reservation and at various locations on the eastern coastal towns and cities of Virginia. Plans were made to take the play on the road to locations as diverse as Omaha, Nebraska to Paris, France, but financial support never materialized.

Origins

The origin tales of certain Native-American societies place them where they were first encountered by Europeans. The Algonquin, of whom Pamunkey is a branch, reflect a different story of creation that has been passed down over time as popular legend that has been widely reprinted.

The Great Earth Mother had two sons. Glooskap was good, wise and creative. Malsum was evil, selfish and destructive.

When their mother died, Glooskap created plants, animals and humans from his mother's body. Malsum instead made poisonous plants and snakes. Malsum grew tired of his good brother and plotted to kill him.

Malsum bragged that he was invincible

Outsized statue of Glooscap.

**Blue clay from a submerged forest
developed during the Holocene period.**

except one thing that could kill him: the roots of the fern plant. Meanwhile he badgered Glooskap to find his vulnerability. As Glooskap could tell no lies, he confided that he could be killed only by an owl feather. Malsum made a dart from an owl feather and killed Glooskap. The power of good is so strong, however, that Glooskap rose from the dead to avenge himself.

Alive again, Glooskap knew that Malsum would continue to plot against him. He had no choice but to destroy Malsum so good would survive and his creatures would continue to live. He went to a stream and attracted his evil brother by saying loudly that a certain flowering reed could also kill him. Glooskap pulled a reed plant out by the roots and flung it at Malsum, who fell to the ground dead.

Paleo-Indian camp.

Malsum's spirit went underground to become a wicked wolf-spirit that torments humans and animals.

Anthropologists believe man first reached America at the start of the **Holocene** period, after the last Ice Age. The Holocene spans the last 11,000 years to the present day. It is also called the Anthropogenesis, or the Age of Man, because it marks his arrival.

Archeology reflects the progressive settlement of aborigines. After the last Ice Age, the first people crossed the Bering Strait and began to spread south and east across America. The distinct fluted characteristics of tools, arrowheads and axe heads found throughout Canada into the

**Mastodon remains from the Archaic
era, found near Nashville, Tennessee.**

Great Plains and onward to the Eastern Woodlands suggest a rapid population growth.

These ancestors, called the Paleo-Indians, acclimated well to their new world by adjusting to unfamiliar weather conditions and adapting to strange new animal and vegetation resources. Mammoths and mastodons roamed freely. Elk, caribou and moose were taken for food. Their bones were shaped into tools and other implements, while their skins provided clothing and shelter.

As climates became warmer, the environment shifted. Woodlands, prairies, floodplains, deserts and forests changed. These changes altered plant and animal life. Mastodons, mammoths, giant ground sloths and other large-bodied plant-eaters began to die off. As they became extinct,

Eastern Woodlands scenario, Archaic era.

so did many of the meat-eaters that subsisted on them. The Alaskan lion, saber-toothed tiger and dire wolf were casualties.

Other species did not become extinct but evolved into smaller forms. For example, the giant bison was gradually replaced by the modern bison. Scientists previously thought that the ancestral American Indians of the Paleo-Indian period hunted these animals into extinction. Today scientists point instead to a period of rapid global warming at the end of the Ice Age. As the climate changed, sea levels rose, growing seasons became longer, and snowfall and rain declined. While many animals could survive these changing conditions by adapting to their altered habitats, larger ones that placed a greater demand on scarce resources.

In response to their changing world, the ancestral American Indians became increasingly efficient at subsisting on a variety of resources. They followed a seasonal and migratory way of life that still depended on gathering and hunting, and their cultures became more technologically advanced.

The end of the Paleo-Indian period, a span of adaptation to the post-Ice Age environment, is known as the **Archaic** era. People began making new kinds of tools for grounding seeds and nuts. They fashioned baskets, nets and fishing tools. They developed new techniques for using tools. Cultural developments among the natives included far-reaching regional trade networks for the exchange of raw materials and food. They also developed specialized occupational skills.

Britannica.com

Clovis points, named for the site found in New Mexico.

The lifestyles of the Paleo-Indian societies had few types of subsistence and settlement patterns and locales. The Archaic period led to the advent of different lifestyles, spreading across the land.

Adaptations made to the changing world of North America were more easily made in some regions than others. Survival was difficult in the deserts, while along the coast the abundant aquatic resources and wildlife afforded more complete lifestyles. Regardless, people exploited the resources at hand.

Some populations evolved from hunting large game to medium and small game while others added more vegetation to their diet. Elsewhere, seafood and a variety of plants became the staples. In most places, the food consisted of vegetables, smaller animals (squirrels, deer, rabbits) and fish.

The Pamunkey area in the Eastern Woodlands offered a variety of foods including nuts, seed-bearing grasses, small game, fish and shellfish. This gathering and hunting way of life lasted in some regions of North America well into the middle and late 19th century. The changes in differing ways of life led to changes in other cultural patterns. Groups of people began to separate from each other by region. The Archaic period people were changing into more complex foraging and hunting cultures, not dominated by any one culture.

Pennsylvania State University

Woolly mammoth was hunted during Clovis complex site era.

The oldest identified Native-American culture is known as the **Clovis** complex, named for a site discovered in 1932, near Clovis, New Mexico. The culture existed from about 11,200 to 10,900 years ago.

These ancient people were big-game hunters and foragers. Anthropological digs on the North American Great Plains suggest that they were efficient hunters of mammoth and bison. Apparently they approached the animals at watering places to ambush them while their movement slowed. One animal would provide meat for a month or more, and dried meat would last for much of the winter. Whenever a mammoth was slaughtered, they took the meat to store for future consumption. The Clovis hunted bison to a greater extent, using their hides, tusks and bones to make possessions and tools for shelter and clothing. They hunted deer and small rabbits as well.

They apparently used wild plants for nutritional, medical and industrial purposes. As a nomadic group that was always on the move, the Clovis used tool kits that were lightweight and easy to transport.

The stones they used for day-to-day household use were precious, fine-grained rock that came from widely

New Mexico State Parks

Visitors to Clayton Lake State Park still find projectile points from Clovis and Folsom eras on a regular basis.

What the Eastern Woodlands probably looked like.

separated outcrops. The most distinctive parts of the tool kit were their fluted projectile points. The typical Clovis point is leaf-shaped, with parallel or slightly convex sides and a concave base. The edges of the base are ground down, probably to prevent the edge from severing the hafting cord (so the hand can hold the point). Eastern variants of Clovis points such as the Ohio, Cumberland or Suwannee points are somewhat fishtailed and narrower. Exactly how these points were hafted is unknown, but the men probably carried a series of points mounted in wooden or bone for shafts that worked loose from the spear shaft once the head was buried in its quarry.

The Clovis became successful hunters, killing mammoth, mastodons and huge bison throughout the Great Plains of North America and northern Mexico. They used bone tools, hammer stones, scrapers and non-fluted projec-

Dwelling typical of the era when Eastern Woodlands tribes began centralized control of satellite groups.

tile points. Their ancestors are believed to have moved south from Alaska, pursuing their the mammoth as their favorite prey.

Following the Clovis is the **Folsom** complex (11,000 - 10,200 years ago). People of this era used fluted projectile points that were smaller and more finely carved in contrast to Clovis points. The bison of their day, now extinct, were almost one-and-a-half times larger than today's bison.

Some 10,000 years ago, several similar hunting-based cultures spanned many parts of North America. These cultures, called Plano, were known chiefly by their similar non-fluted chipped projectile points. The Plano faded out by around 6000 B.C., perhaps blending with other cultures.

Over time, the many Indian settlements developed spe-

Serpent Mound State Memorial Photo Gallery

Ohio Valley burial mound.

cific identities. By the end of the Folsom period, North America had a myriad of different cultures, languages and societies. Some developed into complex, socio-political systems, graduating from nomadic roaming to sedentary settlements in permanent villages. They were a far cry from the ignorant savages portrayed in American movies and TV serials in the 20th century.

The Indians experimented by trial and error with many North American plants to survive in the woodlands. They used fire, manufactured pottery, and engaged in trade between friendly societies.

The **Formative** period began sometime between 3,000 and 5,000 years ago. Native societies were becoming remarkably complex. In some cases, people in various geographical regions engaged in full-time agriculture, lived in cities of 10,000 or more people, and elevated their leaders literally as well as figuratively. In the ancient city of

**Area traditionally known as Powhatan's mound
on the Pamunkey reservation.**

Cahokia, leaders were considered incarnations of deities and lived on top of large mounds hundreds of feet high.

In the southwestern United States, societies organized together under the name Anasazi. They erected multi-storied apartment complexes, built roads to connect their towns with each other, and engaged in long-distance trading with the diverse cultures now spread across the North American continent.

New features of subsistence, technology and society began to appear in different parts of the New World. Settlements became prolific and larger. Many settlements were located in areas where two or more environments came together. By settling in such locations, people could use a wider variety of resources without having to relocate their homes. Over time, small camps were established as satellite camps. Eventually each major community was surrounded by lesser camps, and forms of social and political relations emerged between them.

With these changes evolved a class system differentiating elites, nobles, commoners, poor and vagabonds. Some places even had professional guilds.

Around 1000 B.C., important innovations took hold in societies in the Eastern Woodlands: pottery manufacture, farming, and burials under funerary mounds.

In eastern North America, many groups began to supplement their gathering and hunting diets by the planting native seedlings, and thus arose the first farming efforts. The seeds of sunflowers as well as marsh elder and gourd were taken from the wild along riverbanks long before they were grown as farm crops.

Colorado Archaeology Society

Ceramic fragments from Protohistoric period.

Congruent with the rise of agricultural farming and greater use of wild resources were social gatherings on a regular basis. There arose a form of barter system for goods and services, and an increase in rites and ceremony, especially concerning burial.

Around 3,000 years ago, in the Midwestern and Southeastern parts of the continent, elaborate burial customs and building burial mounds out of earth were common. The best known of these mound-building cultures were the Adena society of native tribes and the Hopewell group, both from the Ohio Valley. The Adena existed 1000 B.C. to 200 A.D. The Hopewell flourished 300 B.C. to 700 A.D. Not much is known of either except that they shared cultural similarities and co-existed peacefully for centuries.

Further north, European fishing expeditions regularly visited the flourishing fishing grounds off the coast of present-day Canada and New England. These fishers often came ashore to acquire water, food and fuel.

Some suggest that they may have infected the local Indian populations with diseases for which they had little or no genetic immunity.

In the land where the Powhatan Confederacy eventually flourished, in the era known as the Late Woodland era, sea levels had stabilized. Since the fertile soil of the river banks provided ideal conditions, farming became a vital part of their subsistence technology. Their meats came from seasonal hunting expeditions. Fish, shellfish and eel supplemented their diets.

Wikipedia

Unflattering depiction of Pocahontas.

Bones and other items found in excavated communal trash pits give evidence of their dietary habits. The natives of this period buried their refuse in these pits to prevent attracting bears and other night predators. Foraging was still a primary source for food, to supplement agricultural farming efforts. They began growing corn around 900 A.D.

Fish was readily available and made an ideal fertilizer for the new crops. Ceramic pottery, tempered with shell fragments, flourished as well. These early examples of pottery were functional and practical, not decorative. Glazing and painting came later, in the 20th century. Arrowheads, spear points and axe heads were made from the stones found in sparse quantity in the coastal soils. Paint, made from the pucoon plant (also called bloodroot), was likely acquired in trade with other tribes, such as the Tuscarora.

The last period immediately preceding recorded history is the **Protohistoric** era. This era was marked by

Smithsonian Institution

Robert Miles grinding meal. Farming, hunting and fishing became major means of sustenance when the Pamunkey came out of the Protohistoric era, prior to European contact.

the advent of Werowances, or supreme regional chiefs, who may be seen as the equivalent of U.S. governors, albeit ruling a larger area. Werowances oversaw satellite tribes, and in turn were ruled by lesser chiefs.

Wahunsunacoke, born circa 1540, ruled 32 tribes and took the name Powhatan from the town of Powhatan, near present-day Richmond. He inherited six districts of natives, probably from one of his mother's brothers since it was a matriarchal system. Three districts were on the James riverbanks and three were on the York shores.

The alliance of other tribes to this central core probably came about as a mutually agreed upon security measure to protect them from constant raids from aggressive neighboring factions.

Foundation for Advancement of MesoAmerican Studies

Ceramic images made in the Formative era.

Around 1560, Spanish ships from Cuba began coming ashore in Virginia. They took a young native, named him Don Luis, and for the next 10 years kept took him from Mexico City to Madrid. Eventually he was approached by missionaries to guide them in attempts to establish a small settlement, with the purpose of converting the natives to Christianity.

The missionaries foolishly insisted on settling inland from the York, in territory that proved hostile to. Don Luis eventually rejoined his people. When the missionaries' food dissipated they asked the neighboring tribes for help. No doubt seen as tolerated intruders on native land, the missionaries were eventually massacred. In retaliation, the captain of a military expedition hanged five Indians, and hostility towards these newcomers undoubtedly grew.

In 1584 Europeans attempting to settle in Roanoke Island, in present-day North Carolina, struck out with their Indian guides in search of the Chesapeake tribes, with whom they spent the next several months in search of information on lands better suited for colonization. They soon debated attempting to settle a site that was to become known as Jamestown.

www.sonofthesouth.net

Early map of Roanoke Island.

Acknowledgments

I would like to thank the following, without whom this project would not exist: Richard McCluney and his mother Margaret for their memories and cooperative efforts; Joyce Krigsvold, Kevin Brown, Louis Stewart and Russell Bradby for their stories and encouragement; Frank Bradby for transportation on several occasions; James Nickens and Tomas Blumer for background information and historical data; Lou Stancari, photo archivist for the Smithsonian Institute for reproduction permissions; Paula Pannoni for her invaluable work in graphics organization and cover design; and Bill O'Donovan, without whose efforts and patience as editor and agent this work would exist only on my computer.

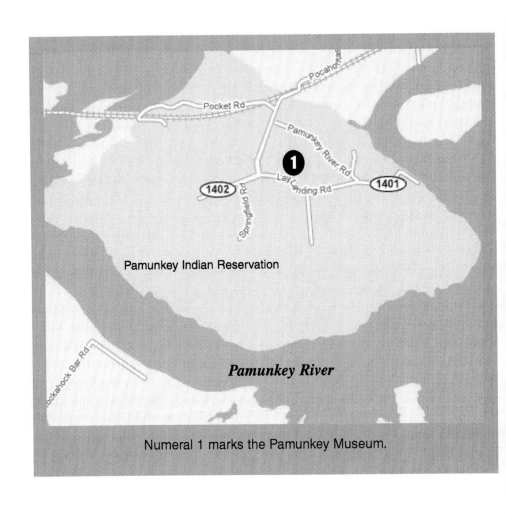

Pamunkey Indian Reservation

Pamunkey River

Numeral 1 marks the Pamunkey Museum.

Made in the USA
Charleston, SC
03 July 2011